Managing Conflict: 50 Strategies for School Leaders

Stacey Edmonson,
Julie Combs, and Sandra Harris

EYE ON EDUCATION
6 DEPOT WAY WEST, SUITE 106
LARCHMONT, NY 10538
(914) 833–0551
(914) 833–0761 fax
www.eyeoneducation.com

Edmonson, Stacey.
  Managing conflict : 50 strategies for school leaders / Stacey
  Edmonson,
Julie Combs, and Sandra Harris.
     p. cm.
  ISBN 978-1-59667-083-9
  1. School management and organization. 2. Conflict management. 3.
Educational leadership. I. Combs, Julie, 1955- II. Harris, Sandra,
1946-
III. Title.
  LB2806.E36 2008
  371.2'07—dc22

                                                      2008003004

10 9 8 7 6 5 4 3 2

Editorial and production services provided by
Hypertext Book and Journal Services
738 Saltillo St., San Antonio, TX 78207-6953 (210-227-6055)

Also Available from EYE ON EDUCATION

BRAVO Principal!
Sandra Harris

What Great Principals Do *Differently*:
15 Things That Matter Most
Todd Whitaker

High-Impact Leadership for High-Impact Schools
Pamela S. Salazar

Get Organized! Time Management for School Leaders
Frank Buck

A School for Each Student:
Personalization in a Climate of High Expectations
Nelson Beaudoin

Lead Me—I Dare You!
Sherrel Bergman and Judith Brough

The Principal as Instructional Leader:
A Handbook for Supervisors, Second Edition
Sally J. Zepeda

What Successful Principals Do!
169 Tips for Principals
Franzy Fleck

Lead With Me:
A Principal's Guide to Teacher Leadership
Gayle Moller and Anita Pankake

The Instructional Leader's Guide to
Informal Classroom Observations
Sally J. Zepeda

Dealing with Difficult Teachers, Second Edition
Todd Whitaker

Meet the Authors

Stacey Edmonson is currently associate professor and director of the Center for Research and Doctoral Studies in Educational Leadership at Sam Houston State University in Huntsville, Texas, where she teaches courses including qualitative research, school law, and instructional theory. Formerly, she served as a teacher, principal and central office administrator in Texas public schools. Her scholarship agenda includes stress and burnout among educators, legal issues in education, and educator ethics. She is also actively engaged in a number of educational leadership organizations at the state and national level.

Julie Combs is currently assistant professor of Educational Leadership at Sam Houston State University. She held a variety of administrative and teaching roles and served as a building administrator for 10 years. In addition to teaching and researching, she consults with school districts on topics such as public relations, communication, and leadership, and conducts program evaluations as an external evaluator. Her current research interests include trust and leadership, the roles and duties of principals, and leadership burnout. She has presented at several national and state conferences and has published numerous journal articles and book chapters.

Sandra Harris is currently associate professor and director of the Center for Doctoral Studies in Educational Leadership at Lamar University in Beaumont, Texas, where she teaches courses in social justice and qualitative research. Formerly, she served as a teacher, principal, and superintendent in public and private schools. Her scholarship agenda includes administrator preparation, K-12 peer harassment, and building relationship-oriented, socially just school environments. She is the author of several other books, including **BRAVO Teacher** and **BRAVO Principal,** and presents at regional, state, and national conferences on these and other related topics.

Table of Contents

Introduction

What Is
Conflict Management Anyway?

Nonstop adversity is the reality of the principal's job.
—Jerry Patterson

Power and organizational politics by their very nature create differing levels of conflict. Generally, even though conflict is influenced by places, issues, and the people involved (Owen & Ovando, 2000), school leaders are often not equipped or trained to resolve conflicts (Barnett, 2004; Storey, 2001). This is unfortunate because the majority of a leader's workday focuses on conflict. Consequently, educators spend a substantial amount of time and energy mediating a variety of circumstances in which individual needs and organizational expectations clash. This has become even more pronounced given the increasing number of groups and stakeholders with whom educational leaders must be involved. For these reasons, Patterson (2007) recently commented that "nonstop adversity is … the reality of the principal's job" (p. 17).

In a 2007 study by Anderson, 255 campus administrators in Texas, 74% reported that they encountered student-related conflict on a routine basis and an additional 18% noted that they dealt with this on a somewhat regular basis. Over half of the administrators indicated that teacher conflict issues occurred at least somewhat regularly. When asked how important they considered conflict management skills, 91% of the administrators indicated that these skills were very important. Yet, over one half of the respondents indicated that they had only had some or even less training in how to handle conflict.

Styles of Conflict Management

As long ago as 1976, Thomas identified two basic dimensions of behavior that produce conflict: trying to satisfy organizational demands, and attempting to meet needs of individual members. The dimension of satisfying organizational needs is considered along an assertive-unassertive continuum, while the dimension attempting to satisfy individual member needs is plotted on an uncooperative to cooperative continuum (see Figure 1).

The framework in Figure 1 examines five styles of conflict management: avoiding, compromising, competing, accommodating, and collaborating. Each of these styles can be effective when applied correctly. Using this framework as a general guide, managing conflict often looks something like this:

 ◆ Avoiding: This is unassertive and uncooperative. The leader ignores conflict. When used at the appropriate time,

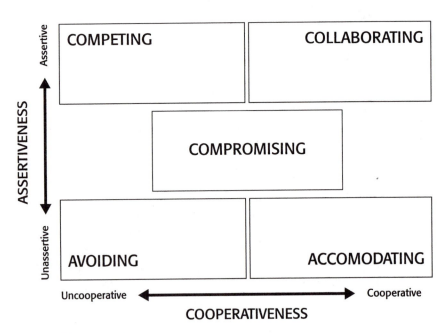

Source: Thomas (n.d.).

Figure 1.   Conflict management styles.

such as in minor issues or when things just need time to "cool down," avoidance can be an effective strategy. When used at the wrong time—when issues are escalating and need to be handled immediately—avoidance can be disastrous! Avoiding-type leaders are often described as "invisible."

- Compromising: This style of conflict management is best described as meeting halfway or finding a middle ground. Compromising works best when demands on both sides of the conflict are reasonable. When issues are not balanced and leaders compromise too often on too many issues, they can be seen as unfocused. Sometimes this is a lose-lose situation as both have to concede.

- Competing: This style is low in cooperation and high in assertiveness. There are times when leaders must step in and make decisions assertively. If the competing style is used too often or in situations where group buy-in is needed, this "My way or the highway!" style can lead to greater conflict.

- Accommodating: Accommodating leaders tend to be highly cooperative, but low in assertiveness. When a leader wants to build good will toward other more important issues, accommodating can be very effective. Some leaders using this style often advise "choose your battles." However, the downside is that this leader can be seen as "namby-pamby" when overusing this as a conflict management strategy.

- Collaborating: This style is high in assertiveness, but also high in cooperation. Leaders who are collaborative, assert themselves with balance, but also work well with others. This style can best be characterized as "win-win."

Other Ways to Manage Conflict

In addition to understanding the styles of conflict management, there are other knowledge and skills that can strengthen a leader's ability to successfully manage conflict. Bagin and Gallagher (2001) suggest that critical skills in conflict management are human relations behaviors that communicate a positive attitude toward others. They recommend the importance of fostering a spirit of collegiality and good will among all stakeholders. In order to do this, leaders must be aware of the importance of communicating in actions, not just words, and being sensitive to perceptions of staff members in the decision-making process. This type of conflict management not only fosters unity among staff, but it decreases conflict through shared decision making, defining instructional issues, pooling resources, identifying appropriate goals, and collaborating on objectives.

Bagin and Gallagher (2001) argued that one strategy for reducing conflict is to implement the concept of quality circles. This process involves six steps: problem identification, problem selection, problem analysis, recommended solutions, management review, and recommendations for implementation. Better communications result in an increased sense of belonging, providing quick feedback, focusing clearly on primary purposes, and improving positive communication to all stakeholders within the school community.

Other strategies for managing conflict include (Hanson, 1991):

- ♦ Expanding needed resources;
- ♦ Having an appeals system in place so that all parties can be heard;
- ♦ Being open to changing interaction patterns between conflicting individuals or groups;
- ♦ Modifying the reward system when an actual or perceived inequity exists;
- ♦ Clarifying ambiguous roles;
- ♦ Consulting with a third party; and
- ♦ Accepting responsibility for the conflict by the leader.

There is little doubt that there are many ways to manage conflict; the issue is how many of these strategies are readily available to the busy administrator throughout the school day.

Our Conflict Management Book

We based this book on our own experiences as school leaders, in conjunction with what we had read and studied regarding conflict management. At the same time, we considered what we heard from other leaders regarding the conflicts they faced daily in their jobs as superintendents, principals, and teacher leaders and how they dealt with these issues. As we integrated all of this information, we began to develop our own patterns of understanding conflict that may help individuals manage the challenging, conflict-ridden job of school leader. We also agree with Lencioni (2007)—conflict, when managed properly, aids school leaders in maintaining highly productive teams leading to stronger organizations. In other words, we want to emphasize that conflict, when it is managed wisely, is an essential resource for the development of the whole school.

We all know the classic Simon and Garfunkel song, "50 Ways to Leave your Lover." We do not want to be trite, but if leaders follow the strategies in this book, they will have at least "50 ways to run for cover"! More importantly, we believe these 50 strategies will help leaders do more than survive conflict. We believe school leaders will actually thrive in conflict and lead their campuses to greater growth. We have also included reflective questions to guide readers in self-evaluating the conflict management strategies used most often and to encourage the use of other strategies. The 50 strategies are divided into three sections: Understanding Conflict Strategies, Developing Proactive Strategies, and Fine-Tuning Your Skills.

Strategies to handle conflict management, from avoiding to collaborating, are implemented throughout the school day. However, too often, we see harried, tired leaders who turn a blind eye to conflicts and just give up, give in, and let "she who speaks the loudest or latest have her way." We believe the following strategies in this conflict management guide will be a resource that will provide teachers, principals, superintendents, and other school leaders the direction to not give up, the wisdom to know when to give in, and the strength to give it your best!

Section I

Understanding Conflict Strategies

Before you can begin to manage conflict appropriately, you must identify basic strategies for understanding conflict. The 17 strategies that follow, while not an exhaustive list, provide you with a deeper knowledge of understanding conflict strategies. After you read each one and respond to the reflective questions, you will be a leader who is better equipped to manage conflict at your school!

1
Learn Who to Trust

Trust men and they will be true to you;
treat them greatly and they will show themselves great.
— Ralph Waldo Emerson

Sometimes leaders are too trusting. We want to believe in the best of everyone and we trust everyone equally. This often leads to conflict as we fail to supervise as completely as we should. On the other hand, we might be inclined to trust no one. Oops, another mistake. Trusting no one also leads to conflict because we hold on too tightly to all decision making. As Blattner said, "a person who trusts no one, can't be trusted" (www.quotations.com). So, what do we do? Trust everyone indiscriminately? Or trust no one? Wise leaders learn to discern who can be trusted and who cannot be trusted. We pay close attention to those around us. We notice the motivation of those around us: who is motivated to know the truth or who is motivated to win a conflict and always get his or her way. We observe who is honest and who exaggerates.

Trust others, but with discernment. When leaders trust and people live up to this expectation, the level of trust grows throughout the campus. When leaders do not trust others (but should), the leadership itself will not be trusted. Leaders must be willing to allow others to earn their trust, all the while remembering that everyone on the school campus is a learner! Doesn't this make the leader somewhat vulnerable? Absolutely! Nevertheless, being vulnerable comes with the territory. Be observant and discerning and you will trust wisely. In so doing, a climate will be created that allows conflicts to be managed with wisdom. Years ago, my grandmother gave me good advice. She said, "It is better to trust wisely and be proven right, than not to trust anyone and be proven wrong."

Reflect:

1. Who are the people with whom you work that you trust?
2. Why?
3. Who are the people on campus who have not earned your trust?
4. In general, are you too trusting?
5. Are you not trusting enough?

Remember, learn who to trust

Be observant and discerning and you will trust wisely.

2
Agree to Disagree

If two men agree on everything,
you may be sure that one of them is doing the thinking.
— Lyndon B. Johnson

Leaders must be able to agree to disagree in some instances. This allows us to disagree without taking issues personally or holding a grudge. However, when we disagree with someone, our natural tendency is to do everything we can to convince the other person that *they* are wrong and *we* are right. For example, before I became a principal, I had been a reading teacher. One year, my school was assigned a teacher who approached the teaching of reading very differently than what I had preferred as a teacher. Her reading techniques certainly fell within appropriate reading strategies and guidelines; she was well-liked by parents and her students made reading progress. Still, the first year that she worked in our school, we found ourselves often arguing about the best ways to teach reading. If we had continued to expend our energies convincing one another that one of us was right and the other was wrong—we would have been in constant conflict. Instead, we finally agreed to disagree respectfully. Not only did this prevent conflict, but it also resulted in an important lesson for me: just because the strategies or teaching styles might differ from those that I had preferred as a teacher did not mean they were less effective. In fact, there is a big difference between something being wrong and something not being the way I would have done it. Sometimes, we have to agree to disagree.

Disagreeing can be a very powerful component that leads to constructive change. If we all saw everything in exactly the same way, there would be no progress, as well as no variety. Janis and Mann (1977) called this "group think." While group think is generally without conflict (and that is good), it can actually be a paralyzing problem (and that is bad)! After all, William Wrigley, Jr. pointed out that if there is too much agreement, someone is "unnecessary." This illustrates that our goal should not be a climate where everyone agrees. In fact, a healthy climate is one where people *can* disagree without resorting to personal attacks or arguments.

Reflect:

1. Do you always have to be right?
2. Do those who disagree with you always have to be wrong?
3. When should you agree to disagree?
4. When someone disagrees with you, do you feel attacked?
5. When you are wrong, how do you feel?
6. What do you do?

Remember, agree to disagree

One goal on a campus should be that it is a place where people **can** disagree.

3
Agree to Agree

My idea of an agreeable person is a person who agrees with me.
— Benjamin Disraeli

A new dress code has been adopted into policy. Students must tuck in their shirts. One of the assistant principals just does not consider this important. In fact, he insists that the relationships with the boys are far more important than a tucked-in shirt. However, the board has adopted the policy and you, as the principal, are obligated to adhere to this policy and to enforce it consistently on campus. One day, this becomes a heated issue in an administrative team meeting. As principal, you completely agree that relationships are important. However, to disregard or be inconsistent with this policy will actually create discord among students, teachers, and parents.

The leader's challenge is not to argue about the correctness of the board policy, but instead to remind everyone on the team of the importance of implementing this policy in a way that reduces potential conflicts due to inconsistency. In other words, before the meeting is over, everyone must agree to agree on how the policy will be enforced to keep the shirts tucked in, but also to do so in a way that does not negatively impact relationships with students. The principal in this case stated the board policy at the beginning of a staff meeting. Then he directed the conversation toward *implementation* of the policy. He reminded the team of the school's mission statement which emphasized treating all students with respect. He then restated the challenge in this way: "How will we implement the new dress code policy while treating all students with respect?" Soon, instead of debating the policy, administrative team members agreed on several strategies, such as speaking to students privately and supporting faculty in being consistent.

In most circumstances, the leader's job is to find a way to get everyone on board and moving in the same direction. While you do not want to be dictatorial, there are circumstances when agreement across the board is necessary. Agreeing to agree does not mean there is no room for input—it just means that there is only room for *some* input. In the case of this dress code issue, the "wiggle room" was in *how* the policy would be implemented.

Reflect:

1. Can you identify an "agree to agree" situation on your campus?
2. How did you handle it then?
3. How might you have handled it differently?
4. How do you deal with policies that you strongly oppose?

Remember, agree to agree

When you agree to agree, the flexibility lies in the solution.

4
Know When to
Be Competitive

If you make every game a life and death proposition,
you're going to have problems.
For one thing, you'll be dead a lot.
—Dean Smith

Being competitive is often a conflict style that is used by individuals who are assertive and power oriented. These individuals are often viewed as uncooperative because they appear to be more concerned with winning the conflict than with solving the conflict in the best interests of everyone. In other words, these people would fight over the last piece of cake on the Titanic! This style does not allow for input; instead, competitors act alone and use their power or status to achieve their desires.

On the other hand, despite the forceful nature of being competitive, there are times when this style is appropriate in managing conflict—both to prevent and reduce conflicts. When a decision needs to be made quickly, this style will cut through conflict to determine a course of action. In addition, sometimes, when an important decision needs to be made on the campus regarding enforcing difficult rules or making hard decisions regarding resource allocation, the competitive style may be the best strategy.

Reflect:

1. When do you need to use your power or status to achieve the desired outcome?

2. How often have you used this style in the past month?

3. What were the circumstances?

Remember, know when to be competitive

The competing style is sometimes appropriate in managing conflict, especially when an important decision needs to be made quickly or when enforcing difficult rules.

5
Know When
to Compromise

Don't compromise yourself. You are all you've got.
— Janis Joplin

I recently talked with a newly appointed principal who is committed to changing the dress code policy to require all students to wear uniforms at her school. The president of the local Parent-Teacher Association, a highly respected individual in the school community, was completely against uniforms. After meeting with the PTA president on several occasions, the principal compromised her original goal. She settled on a more specific, more stringent dress code policy in lieu of uniforms. She still felt that her goal of uniforms was important, but it was not worth the potential conflict it could cause in the school community without adequate support.

Preventing and reducing conflicts by compromise is a common strategy. Unlike the competing individual, the compromiser is willing to give up some of his position, but not all of it. At the same time, the leader who compromises must know where to draw the line or this style of conflict management is often seen as giving in and results in a lose-lose outcome. This leader can sometimes be viewed as one without a strong vision or the courage to stand up for what is right. Consequently, leaders must ask themselves, "How far can I go to reach the desired outcome while trying to minimize conflict and maintaining my integrity?"

Let's face it, some conflicts are best settled with a healthy compromise. Leaders must pick their battles carefully and realize that sometimes giving in is NOT giving up. Compromising may, in fact, allow a leader to build a relationship today that will be helpful in addressing other, more important issues later on.

Reflect:

1. Describe a circumstance where you compromised your position?
2. What was the desired goal?
3. What was the solution?
4. Did the solution move you closer to that ultimate goal?

Remember, know when to compromise

Ask yourself: How much can I give in without giving up?

6
Know When
to Collaborate

If we are going to seize the promise of our times and educate
our children so they can keep their dreams alive,
we must all work together.
—Bill Clinton

Collaboration is most effective when it is inquiry based. This means that those involved enter the negotiations curious to find a creative, best answer for the circumstance. All parties commit to trying to understand the other's perspective and to remove their own personal bias. For example, consider that there is a major scheduling problem at High School A because the school board has adopted a new policy that no longer allows athletes, band, and pep-squad members to meet during the seventh period elective hour. The coaches, band leaders, parents, and students are upset and view the issue from their perspective.

The principal must support the board policy and must maintain positive relationships with his faculty, students, and parents. Using a collaborative inquiry style, a committee representing each of the interest groups is formed. Together, they work until a solution is created that satisfies the board's commitment to a more academic use of the school day and also satisfies the coaches, students, and parents. By not giving up, and by working together, the collaborative approach helps everyone involved keep their focus on the main goal, and still satisfies the needs and interests of others in the district. The collaborative style takes time and should be applied in situations that are important. Leaders cannot use this style all the time or others will grow frustrated with the time it takes to arrive at a decision.

Preventing and reducing conflicts by being collaborative is both cooperative and assertive. In this case, leaders work with as many parties as possible who are involved in the conflict or in the potential conflict. Everyone involved in the collaboration understands that there is an issue to be solved and all parties agree to work toward the best solution for everyone. This level of conflict strategy requires a high level of trust, because all involved must put aside their specific interest for the common good. There must be an open sharing of the circumstances so that everyone understands the issue as completely as possible. Such is the challenge of collaboration as a tool for conflict management.

Reflect:

1. When was the last time that you led a collaborative effort in managing conflict?
2. What solution was created?
3. How did the solution come about? How much time was invested?
4. What do you find most difficult about being collaborative?

Remember, know when to collaborate

Collaboration is most effective when it is inquiry-based.

7
Know When
to Avoid or Not to Avoid

*Leadership is being visible when things are going awry
and invisible when they are working well.*
—Tom Peters

To be involved or not to be involved? I wonder if Hamlet was really thinking of conflict when he reflected so famously "To be or not to be ..." Probably not. However, this important question must be answered when considering conflict. If the issue is minor, or if involved individuals simply need to calm down and put some distance between the issue of concern, you make the right decision when you decide to avoid being involved. We have all observed issues that de-escalated or even disappeared after a good night's rest. In this case, "not to be" is the correct answer. In fact, you might actually make things worse if you insert yourself into a minor problem that should be handled by the individuals themselves.

However, if you see that an issue is becoming more serious, more heated, and perhaps involving more individuals, then the right answer to this famous question is "to be" involved. You must choose to involve yourself in helping to resolve the conflict.

To help you decide whether you should ignore the issue or get involved, the primary concern should be the nature of the issue and its importance to the goals of education. We suggest that you consider the following questions:

- How does it affect the students?
- Is the safety or welfare of students involved?
- How many individuals are involved in the conflict?

- ◆ How long has the conflict lasted?
- ◆ Is the conflict exacerbating in intensity?
- ◆ Is the conflict interfering with the work of the school?

Reflect:

1. Describe the last conflict on your campus that you chose to ignore.
2. Did this conflict become resolved without your help?
3. Did it become more intense?
4. Can you describe a conflict where you became involved but later thought that you should have avoided involvement?
5. Describe the last conflict on your campus where you chose to involve yourself.
6. Did your involvement defuse the conflict?
7. What did you do?
8. Generally, are you more likely to avoid getting involved or more likely to get involved with conflicts?

Remember, know when to avoid or not to avoid

Consider the potential of the conflict to interfere with the work of the school.

8
Know When to Accommodate

I always wanted to be somebody—
I guess I should have been more specific.
—Lily Tomlin

Sometimes conflict arises because leaders are more concerned about keeping people happy than they are about making decisions that are in the best interests of the organization. This is most likely to happen when leaders say "yes" too often. While it is often fun in the beginning to work for those who say yes to your every request, once you realize that they say yes to every request from everyone, the honeymoon is over. Conflicts often arise when this happens. After all, are you saying yes because you think it is the right answer for the organization, or are you saying yes because you fear if you say "no" you will create an enemy? Saying yes too easily and too often leads to as much conflict as it does when you never say yes at all.

On the other hand, when a conflict is over minor, unimportant issues, an accommodating strategy is a quick way to resolve a situation and maintain relationships with those involved. The accommodation style often allows you to build good will toward other more important issues. It is okay to be a teddy bear sometimes, but be careful not to use this strategy too often or you will be viewed as namby-pamby because you give in or give up too easily.

Reflect:

1. What was the main issue in the last conflict where you were more accommodating?

2. What influenced your decision—the level of the concern, maintaining the relationship, or a lack of courage on your part?

3. When was the last time that you were not accommodating, but should have been?

Remember, know when to accommodate

Decide if the conflict is over minor, fairly unimportant issues in the long run.

9
Know When to Implement a Temporary Fix

*No one will thank you for taking care of
the present if you have neglected the future.*
—Joel Barker

Conflicts can occur when a problem is large and complex and there is not time to brainstorm the most suitable arrangement. For example, a teacher leaves in the middle of the year, and you must choose to fill the slot with an unqualified permanent substitute. Meanwhile, you are continuing the search to find and recruit the right individual for this classroom as soon as possible. Students and parents are concerned. Your job is to convince those concerned that this is a temporary solution. One way to do this is to communicate that you understand that this is a Band-Aid which does not solve their concern, but allows you time to recruit a highly qualified teacher to fill this position.

Sometimes as a leader, you simply need time for the right solution to be put in place. Although the temporary solution is really just a Band-Aid, it allows you the needed time to reach a more satisfactory solution. Here is where that foundation of trust that you have established will provide you support with these faculty, parents, and students.

Reflect:

1. When was the last "Band-Aid" solution you had to implement?

2. What steps did you follow to get the support of concerned individuals?

3. Consider your campus today, how many Band-Aids are in place?

Remember, know when to implement a temporary fix

A Band-Aid can provide needed time to reach a more satisfactory solution, but keep working toward a more lasting solution.

10
Know When to
Talk it Out

*If an educator handles conflict the same way an
untrained layperson would, the educator is not a true professional.*
—John Novak

Educator John Novak (2005) suggests that inviting leaders are committed to finding ways to deal with conflict by following the Rule of the Six C's. The emphasis here is that leaders should make every effort to deal with conflict at the lowest emotional level and the least time-consuming and energy-consuming manner. The six C's in the order that they are typically followed include Concern, Confer, Consult, Confront, Combat, and Conciliate.

The act of showing concern is the first step in the conflict management process. This happens when the leader steps back to reflect on what is occurring and makes a decision regarding possible actions to follow. It may be that the leader decides to be minimally involved and shows concern by simply following the progress of the conflict. It may be that the leader shows concern by stepping up the level of involvement.

After reflecting with concern on a possible conflict, the next stage in the Rule of the Six C's (Novak, 2005) is to confer—in other words, to officially talk it out. In order for a conference to be most meaningful, the leader must have established a reputation for respectful relationships. One way that you initiate a time to confer is by simply letting the individual know that you want to talk with them.

Consider the case of a department head who wields such a heavy hand that teachers do not want to work with her. As the leader of the campus, you reflect on this concern and decide that you must get involved. In so doing, you decide to meet with the team leader to confer about the situation.

The meeting between you and the team leader is casual, in private, and held with self-control. Your purpose in this meeting is to address the conflict issue, discover why conflict is occurring, and identify a possible course of action. The goal is for the person around whom the conflict revolves (in this case the department head) to voluntarily give verbal agreement with what you are requesting her to do. The conference is handled with respect and the issue is addressed in an open, candid manner. The individual is given an opportunity to share her concerns about the issue. Perhaps by conferring about the issue new information will come to light which may change the possible course of action.

After the conference has occurred, it is the leader's responsibility to observe closely to be sure that the appropriate changes requested and agreed upon at the meeting have taken place. If not, then the process escalates to a more formal consultation or even a confrontation.

Reflect:

1. How does the faculty know of your concern when you choose not to get involved?

2. Think back on the most recent issues on your campus; did you take time to reflectively determine your level of involvement? If not, what happened?

3. What was the last conflict issue that you chose to address simply by conferring with the individual?

4. What resolution was decided upon?

5. In retrospect, do you feel that this was the appropriate level of action?

Remember, know when to talk it out

When a leader decides to confer, it must be done with self-control and the issue addressed in an open, candid manner.

ॐॐॐ

11
Know When to Confront

In the confrontation between the stream and the rock, the stream wins—
not through strength, but through persistence.
—Anonymous

Consider again the tyrannical department head. As leader on the campus, it is your responsibility to become more specific when you see that an informal conference did not result in changed behavior. Now, it is time for a formal act of directed conflict management and you decide to meet and confront the concern. At the meeting, you discuss the issue again and remind the department head about the previous agreement to be less controlling with the other teachers. Respectfully and calmly, you note that the agreed-upon actions have not occurred. You invite her to provide feedback and encourage her to identify possible suggestions. You should be prepared to provide directives if her ideas are sparse. Novak (2005) explains that at this point, you should document the actions in the past that led to the meeting and the outcome of the meeting.

While an important goal is to share ideas that result in positive changes for student learning, another, more fundamental goal at this point is to reduce the level of conflict and provide specific directions. You should review what happened during the meeting. Did you make your expectations clear? Did you give the department head an opportunity to share her ideas and point of view? Did any new information come to light? Did the session identify reasonable, doable actions that may reduce the conflict?

As the meeting ends, do not hesitate to verbalize that you will be observing to see that the solutions are implemented. Reiterate your expectation that the department head follow through with the agreed-upon action.

If there is no change in behavior, the leader must move up the level of involvement and schedule a direct, no-nonsense confrontation. While this must be done respectfully, the leader must be very clear that the situation must be resolved. What was agreed upon prior has not occurred. As leader, it is your responsibility to see that the behavior changes, and it is perfectly appropriate for you to state this very clearly, both verbally and in writing. Remember to use self-control and keep your voice evenly modulated. After stating what must be done to resolve the situation, let her know that further action will follow. In other words, in dealing with the recalcitrant department head, state plainly that if the behavior does not change, future action will be taken. Remind the individual that this confrontation will be documented in her personnel file (and provide her with a copy). Novak (2005) suggests that when a conflict has moved to the confrontation stage, the leader should be careful that the ultimatum issued is indeed something that he or she has the documentation to support and the authority to implement.

Reflect:

1. Reflect on conflicts on your campus. Is there an example where you escalated to confrontation too quickly?
2. What might you have done instead?
3. Have you spoken with others in confidence for help with suggestions which you have not yet considered?

Remember, know when to consult and confront

Use self-control and keep your voice evenly modulated, regardless of the level of conflict.

12
Know When to
Go to Battle

Error of opinion may be tolerated where reason is left free to combat it.
—Thomas Jefferson

Novak's Rule of the Six C's for handling conflict states that after we show concern, confer, consult, and confront, then we actually need to combat. This means that you have tried everything you know to try to resolve a situation that must be solved. The concern cannot be ignored. For example, in dealing with a stubborn department head who refuses to change in spite of your reasoning and directives, no one individual is worth the risk of losing good teachers. Even if teachers do not leave, we all know that when people work in an affirming, positive climate, everyone gains. After all, it is the leader's responsibility to be concerned about actions that create disagreement within the department and this is likely to spill negatively over into the whole campus. Thus, in these types of situations it is time for you as the leader to go to battle to handle the conflict.

Remember, the combat is not with the individual, but rather the battle is with the actions that are taking place. When you have respectfully and carefully implemented all of Novak's previously suggested steps: concern, confer, consult, confront, and still the issue is not resolved, you must follow through with future actions. In this case, you may need to replace the department head and make a reassignment. Always remember to treat the individual involved with dignity and respect. It is likely that at this point, the whole issue has become emotional, and perhaps known among the faculty, so you must work diligently at maintaining a calm demeanor. Maintain confidentiality. Be cautious about what is said about the situation (both verbally and nonverbally).

Many times the results of combat, or going to battle, in conflict situations can be unpredictable. Therefore, before resorting to combat, think through the whole issue as cautiously and as thoughtfully as possible before taking action. Be sure that you have exhausted all appropriate possible solutions. Be sure that you have viewed the situation from as many perspectives as possible. When taking combat action be sure that you have the support of your supervisors before acting. In other words, be prepared.

Reflect:

1. When considering the need to "combat," have you exhausted other possibilities?
2. Is there something that you have missed or overlooked?
3. Is it possible to view the situation from another perspective?
4. What was the most recent issue on your campus where you had to resort to combat action?
5. What resulted from this action? What were the benefits? The costs?

Remember, know when to go to battle

When taking combat action be sure that you have the support of your supervisors. Be prepared for the unexpected.

13
Know How to Conciliate

*If you want to make peace,
you don't talk to your friends. You talk to your enemies.*
—Moshe Dayan

As a leader, much of your job seems to focus on solving conflicts. In fact, Novak's Rule of Six C's emphasizes that despite the fact that you may have done everything from show concern to engage in combat strategies to resolve a conflict, it is your responsibility to "return to a state of normalcy" (Novak, 2005, p. 56). Now, it is time to be conciliatory. To conciliate in this case means you must follow another Rule of the Cs: Be Careful. This means that

- ♦ you are careful to do nothing to keep the battle going;
- ♦ you are careful what you say to others;
- ♦ you are careful to give individuals involved some space;
- ♦ you are careful to be respectful with all involved;
- ♦ you are careful to not continue talking about what has happened; and
- ♦ you are careful to not hold a grudge.

In other words, to conciliate means that after you have done all that you can to address and quell the conflict, it is your responsibility to restore the campus to a state of calm and normalcy and to allow the issue to rest.

Reflect:

1. What strategies did you follow to return your campus to peace after combat over an issue?

2. What did you learn from the conflict?
3. What do you wish you had done differently?
4. What, if anything, should you say publicly?

Remember, know how to conciliate

It is the leader's responsibility to create calm on the campus after a conflict.

14
Understand Your Upbringing

Psychiatry enables us to correct our faults
by confessing our parents' shortcomings.
— Laurence J. Peter

How did your parents model conflict resolution? By reflecting on the conflict styles modeled by our first teachers, we can gain insight into our own conflict management styles.

Sally's mom and dad rarely addressed conflict in an open way. Her mom would blow up in a rage and then not speak to anyone for several days. After days of the "silent treatment," her mom would act as if nothing had happened. Her dad retreated from the conflict and did not mention the situation ever again. Instead, he internalized the conflict. He felt he was responsible for causing the conflict. Sally often felt her dad was aloof, nonresponsive, and uncaring. Actually, her dad often experienced depression and would sometimes drink to numb the pain.

Joe's parents were both demonstrative and highly expressive people. They laughed much and fought with great gusto. The argument, like a storm, would be fierce and then quickly pass over.

Think back to your first models of conflict. Today, do you tend to avoid conflict or face it head on? Perhaps you even cause conflict sometimes! If you witnessed bouts of rage, you may avoid conflict at all costs. The sight of angry people may frighten you. Because anger is a common emotion that accompanies conflict, think back to how anger was handled in your home. Were you allowed to express anger? What happened when you were angry?

Now, consider how you react when faced with an expressively angry person. Do you listen? Do you interrupt? Do you feel the need to defend yourself? Do you leave the room or walk away? Do you feel responsible? Do you place blame on them? Perhaps you focus on how their faces turn red and their nostrils flare!

We learn by models; our parents or grandparents were our early models. We observed family conflicts and were involved in many of our own. Now, you may find yourself avoiding conflict or confronting conflict, much like one of your parents. By knowing your early influences and identifying your most common conflict reactions, you can understand the effective and not so effective ways of managing conflict.

Reflect:

1. What happened in your home when you or a sibling expressed anger?
2. What were the conflicts like in your home between your parents, your siblings, and your extended family members?
3. How did your family act the next day after a conflict?

Remember, understand your upbringing

Identify the conflict styles that were modeled for you as a child. Consider how these styles influence you today.

15
Find the Facts

Get your facts first, and then
you can distort them as much as you please.
—Mark Twain

Often, a conflict occurs when facts are assumed and not communicated. Consider the following conflict: A student reports to his parent that Mrs. Jones, his teacher, ignores his requests for help. Moreover, the student has several failing grades and feels that his teacher does not care. The following day, the parent calls Mrs. Jones. The parent is angry and communicates her dissatisfaction with the teacher's apparent lack of help. The teacher, surprised, reacts defensively. The parent, not satisfied, contacts an administrator. Such conflicts revolve around the lack of agreement about what happened and why.

Your role, after listening, is to gather the facts that are relevant to the situation. The parent, student, and teacher often have a unique perspective of what happened. As it turned out, the teacher had regular tutoring sessions, but the student did not share the information with his parent. The teacher was willing to help, but she would not help the student during a test. The teacher cared, but did not know the student very well. The conflict was the result of misunderstanding.

How you gather facts is important. Time, listening, and objectivity are essential. Speak with each person one-on-one. Probe gently and calmly; use caution in how you ask the questions. Others will be less willing to share facts with you if they perceive that you are closed-minded, angry, or judgmental. Teachers need your help to understand why you are gathering the facts and your role in supporting faculty as well as students. If you have demonstrated confidentiality and genuine care in the past, you are more likely to get closer to the truth. Recognize that some will dispute the facts, perhaps subconsciously, to protect themselves. After you have talked with each person, map out your understanding of the facts.

Even with the best detective skills, you will not know all the facts. After you have some information, decide if a group meeting or individual contact would be best for facilitating understanding. It will depend on the individuals and the seriousness of the conflict. Share your understanding of the facts and find areas of agreement. With a focus on resolution, agree where you can, agree to disagree, and move on to resolution.

Reflect:

1. Do you think that teachers expect you to defend their actions, no matter what?

2. How do you gather facts with situations involving student conflicts?

3. How might you help teachers understand the fact-finding stage of conflict management?

Remember, find the facts

Often, conflicts revolve around the lack of agreement about what happened and why. If you have demonstrated confidentiality and genuine care in the past, you are more likely to get closer to the truth.

16
Be Aware of Nonverbal Cues

Silence is the element in which great things fashion themselves.
—Maurice Maeterlinck

Many times, silence can speak louder than words. It is often not what is said that makes an impression, but how it is said. Take, for example, the person who comes to you to explain a problem he is having with his job but does so in a harsh or condescending tone, or stands (while you sit) with arms folded across his chest, eyes directed at the ceiling, and a sneer on his face. Regardless of what comes out of his mouth, it is clear that he is not happy.

Even small children can notice nonverbal cues. Have you ever made a child apologize, only to hear a "sorry" that was so overshadowed by nonverbal cues that even the family dog knew it was not sincere? Nonverbal cues are a huge part of communication. Take care not to overlook the message that your body language, tone of voice, and eye contact can send. These are windows into your true feelings, and they can easily convey a message that conflicts with the words coming from your mouth or supports them.

In the same way, nonverbal cues can also send a positive message. Consistent eye contact, a smile, or nodding your head while someone else is speaking can allow you to acknowledge that person's feelings and viewpoints without even uttering a word. Use this powerful tool to emphasize your message. Additionally, be careful that nonverbal cues are not a source of additional conflict by exposing an insincere attitude.

Reflect:

1. What sort of nonverbal cues can you look for in a conflict situation?

2. What are some ways you can address nonverbal cues?

3. Examine your own nonverbal cues when communicating with others.

4. What message are you sending to other parties with your nonverbal cues?

5. How can you use nonverbal cues in a positive way?

Remember, be aware of nonverbal cues

Become aware of your body language, both positive and negative. Be aware of your own nonverbal cues as well as those of other parties involved in a conflict.

17
Be Careful With Anything Other Than Face-to-Face Discussions

*Better to remain silent and be thought a fool
than to speak out and remove all doubt.*
—Abraham Lincoln

In a world increasingly impacted by technology, there are new forms of communication that have become not only acceptable, but also quite popular. Text messages, for example, are an enormously popular means of communicating among today's young people. One of the keys to communicating effectively is ensuring that your means of communication are appropriate (e.g., telephone, e-mail, letter, memo, face to face). Still, communication is a two-way street. In order for effective communication to take place, the receiver must interpret your message the way you intended it to be interpreted. When the communication is anything other than face to face, the chances of something being misinterpreted increases. In fact, recent studies have shown that in using e-mail, the person sending the message believes he is clearly communicating 78% of the time, and the receiver believes he is correctly interpreting 89% of the time; however, the receiver actually interprets the message correctly only 56% of the time. Thus, both senders and receivers of electronic communication overestimate their ability to communicate effectively via email (Enemark, 2006).

The weakness of any communication attempted via technology is that technology cannot convey emotion. There is no tone of voice, no eye contact, no facial expressions to help communicate both what you are trying to say as well as what you are *not* trying to say. Was your comment sarcastic? Electronic communication has no way to let the sender know this, and a sarcastic remark that is taken literally can have unfortunate consequences. I recently saw an ad in the paper that read "Motorcycle for sale. Ridden only twice ... apparently 'do whatever you want' means something different to my wife." In the same way, the things you "say" in an e-mail or text message may mean something different from what you intended, and with this mode of communication, you have little way of knowing that the message was interpreted correctly. Thus, whenever possible, use face-to-face communication as your first choice for handling conflict.

Reflect:

1. Have you received an e-mail or phone message from someone who was upset or angry about a potential conflict with you?
2. What impact does the way something is communicated have on a conflict situation?
3. When have you sent a written communication in a conflict situation when a conversation would have been more appropriate or effective?
4. What might you have done instead?

Remember, be careful with anything other than face-to-face discussion

Always handle things face-to-face if possible—it eliminates the most potential for miscommunication.

Section II

Developing Proactive Strategies

Now that you have a better understanding of conflict strategies after reading and reflecting on the first 17 strategies, it is time to develop more proactive strategies. After reading and reflecting on the following strategies, you will have 14 additional ways to manage conflict.

18
Build Trust

Ask yourself ... mercilessly: Do I exude trust? E-x-u-d-e, Big word.
Do I smack of "trust"? Think about it. Carefully.
—Tom Peters

The best way to handle conflict is to prevent conflict from happening at all. The first step in preventing conflict is to build trust. According to Covey (2006), building trust is a function of both *character* and *competence*. Character is about integrity, credibility, and our commitment to keeping our word, but it takes competence for those around us to know that we are capable of getting appropriate results. In other words, to build trust as a leader those who work with you must believe that you will do what you say, and that you are also capable of doing what you say!

As the leader of a school district or school campus, everything that you say is filtered through the level of trust that people have in you. In order to be seen as trustworthy, leaders' lives must reflect character that emphasizes at least these three qualities:

- ◆ Honesty
- ◆ Consistency
- ◆ Courage

Unfortunately, most of us, at one time or another, have worked for people who compromised their integrity on a regular basis because they were not honest or because they were not consistent and you could not count on their support. Conflicts occurred on a regular basis because these questions lingered:

- ◆ What is really happening?
- ◆ What will the leader do this time?

- How willing is he to stand up for what is right?
- Does she have the skills needed to follow through?
- Will the current situation return to haunt me?
- Will he follow through?
- Is she talking behind my back?
- What does she *really* think of me?
- Will she try to find out my side of the story?
- Will I be unfairly blamed for something?
- Will my honesty be used against me?
- Why do I feel confused?

On the other hand, when our leaders demonstrate character that is consistently honest and courage that is steadfast, the entire climate of the school is changed to one characterized by trust. It is as though, despite all that goes on at school, there is a safety net that protects us as we work with teachers, students, parents, and the larger community. That safety net is the leaders' character and their competence to lead the organization. When we trust in our leaders' character and their competence, differences of opinion do not become conflicts; instead, they can become opportunities to create a better school.

Reflect:

1. What am I doing to build trust on my campus?
2. How honest am I?
3. How consistent am I?
4. When was the most recent example of my courage?
5. What am I doing to build my skills to be a highly competent leader?

Remember to build trust as a leader

People must believe that you will do what you say. They must also believe you are capable of doing what you say.

శ్రీశ్రీశ్రీ

19
Be Tactful

Definition of tact:
The art of making a point without making an enemy.
— Howard W. Newton

Often surviving conflict is influenced by how we communicate with others. Therefore, learning to be tactful and phrasing our conversation in affirming ways are wonderful strategies to minimize potential conflict. The Ohio State University Extension (2000) identified phrases which either encourage or discourage a free exchange of conversation. For example, when we say the following we might be discouraging conversation:

- You must work together ...
- You will do your ...
- You ought to ...
- It is your responsibility ...
- If I were you ...
- Why don't you ...
- Let me suggest ...
- You are still too new ...
- Why did you ...
- What you need is ...
- We have always done it this way ...
- There, there, it will be all right ...

Instead, we should be saying:

- I think I understand your viewpoint ...
- That's an interesting point ...

- Yes. Mmm hmm …
- Let me see if I understand what you are saying …
- Sounds as though you feel …
- Tell me more about what happened …

Learning what to say, when to say it, and how to say it is essential for leaders. While a parent can call their student lazy, you would be unwise to do so. You have to point out that the student has been so focused on other activities in or outside of the classroom and that his work is not being completed. Specific behaviors recorded (observed data) can help in your communication with the parent. If you respond without tact, the conflict will only escalate. When a board member or parent stops you at the grocery store and complains about a teacher, you should find a tactful way to respond. The grocery store is no place for a personnel discussion. Remember, be tactful. In the words of an anonymous sage: "Never put both feet in your mouth, because then you don't have a leg to stand on!"

Reflect:

1. How often do you communicate in ways that encourage open discussion?
2. How often do you communicate in ways that discourage open discussion?
3. Practice reframing the following sentences in a more tactful, positive way:
   - You never pay attention to what anyone else thinks!
   - You are being unfair!
   - I insist that you do this!
   - I expect this to be on my desk by 8 A.M. tomorrow!

Remember, be tactful

Without tact, the conflict will likely escalate.

೧೯೩೯೩

20
Do What You Say You Will Do

Word gets out that people who do not follow through ...
are more sizzle than steak.
—John Novak

When I was in my first year of teaching, I worked for a principal who appeared to be very good at listening to students, parents, and teachers. His door was always open and he was never too busy to invite one of us into his office to listen to our problems. The problem was that while he did listen, he rarely followed through on what he said he would do.

Another new teacher was having terrible problems with her department chair. This veteran teacher ran the math department with a firm hand and absolutely no new ideas or new strategies were allowed in her department without her knowledge and approval. To make matters worse, her approval was very rare, and usually new ideas were stopped long before they were ever implemented. We had heard that over the past 2 years, several fine teachers had requested transfers because she was so difficult.

Finally, my teacher friend went to the principal and shared her frustration. The principal responded by listening carefully and then promised that he would follow up with the department head. He would talk with her and remind her that her role was that of department head, not "department dictator," he had joked. However, this never happened. As the year proceeded, relationships on the teaching team continued to disintegrate, resulting in another teacher requesting a transfer, and one taking early retirement.

It did not take long for teachers, parents, and students to realize that it did no good to share issues with the principal. It was not enough to listen. All of us on campus wanted leadership from a principal who would follow through with what he said he would do. As it was, faculty members were left on their own when it came to resolving conflict. When the principal was reassigned, there was a sigh of relief throughout the campus.

In writing about invitational leadership, John Novak (2005) commented that the inviting process involves a net that begins with the sender (the principal in this case), moves to the recipient's side (the frustrated teacher), and then comes back to the sender. It is the leader's "ethical responsibility to make sure that what was offered is made available" (p. 53). In order to resolve conflict, leaders must do what they said they would do or it does not take long to realize that they "are more sizzle than steak" (p. 54). Leaders who want to contribute to solving conflict must know the importance of doing what they say they will do.

Reflect:

1. When was the last time someone told you they would do something and then failed to follow through?
2. How did this make you feel?
3. When was the last time you said you would follow up on an issue?
4. Did you do what you said you would do?
5. Did you forget?
6. When you commit to doing something to help solve a conflict, do you write it down or do you have some other strategy that helps you to remember to follow through?

Remember, do what you say you will do

Just listening to a problem does not bring about resolution to the conflict … if you say you will act on it … you must.

❧❧❧

21
Develop Your Skills

When a man says he approves of something in principle,
it means he hasn't the slightest intention of putting it into practice.
—Otto von Bismarck

There are several skills related to the management of conflict. By identifying your strengths in two related skill areas of conflict management, you will be able to pinpoint areas to improve. Consider the skills of communication and collaboration.

During your next meeting or presentation, observe the audience. Do you see signs of confusion, agreement, or attentiveness? Frequently, conflict results from miscommunication and misinformation. By understanding and sharing the information that individuals want and need to be successful, you can help to alleviate potential conflict.

Often, people become frustrated when they cannot get an answer to a question; some adults prefer not to ask questions or to run the risk of looking ignorant. Sometimes the questions are simple—where is the front door to this school? Sometimes the questions are complex—why did you not select my child for the gifted program?

How can you organize and provide access to accurate information? Consider asking those who answer the phones to create a list of frequently asked questions. Collect the questions and answers, and share these in notebooks by the phone or on an updated Web site. Help teachers understand the importance of repeating information about grading practices and student assignments on a regular basis. Once is not enough! Consider sharing the information in multiple formats including print, announcements, e-mail, and Web sites. Do not forget to keep your informal communicators such as parents, volunteers, and custodians informed, too. By assessing and improving your communication skills, specifically in the area of sharing information, you prevent potential conflicts.

A second skill related to conflict management is that of collaboration. Obviously, individuals committed to working together are likely more willing to work out conflicts. By developing your skills in collaborative leadership, you become a model for collaboration. When you specifically discuss your expectations for teamwork, teachers will understand what they need to do. For example, if you want to improve your students' achievement, examine the levels of teacher collaboration across grade levels and subject areas. Do you expect teachers to collaborate about instructional strategies? How often? What specifically should teachers discuss at these meetings? Do teachers have the skills to be effective group members and group leaders? Do teachers share the various leadership roles in the school or does a small group of teachers continue in these roles? When you improve and model effective collaboration skills, you create an environment where conflict is more likely to be addressed and resolved.

Reflect:

1. What are your strengths as a communicator? What areas could you improve?
2. How frequently do you model collaboration for the teachers (e.g., sharing with other administrators, training others to lead groups, serving on committees as an active participant, working with versus against parents)?

Remember, develop your skills

You can alleviate potential conflicts when you share the information that individuals want and need to be successful.

22
Use Policy

There are two great rules of life, the one general and the other particular.
The first is that everyone can in the end, get what he wants,
if he only tries. That is the general rule. The particular rule is
that every individual is, more or less, an exception to the rule.
—Samuel Butler

Have you ever played a board game with someone who insisted on consulting the rule book? Have you played with someone who conveniently changed the rules to his advantage? The rules serve as a measure of fairness, something objective (at least in theory) to guide the resolution of our disagreements about who wins. Consequently, you have likely experienced others changing the rules or redefining the rules to meet their situation.

In schools, conflicts often arise in situations where rules are fuzzy or have been poorly communicated. When you think about conflict management, consider the role of rules in the conflict. Using rules can facilitate conflict; using rules can escalate conflict. The wise administrator knows how to use rules or policies to encourage agreement.

Step 1: Identify the rules or policies related to the conflict. Sometimes the conflict is about a policy or a misunderstanding of the policy. Sometimes a conflict can occur because there is no policy, rule, or consistent practice. Many of our laws, policies, and rules were developed as a way to correct deficiencies and prevent future conflicts.

Step 2: After you have identified the involved policy (or lack of), gather each person's understanding or misunderstanding of the situation and policy (if applicable). Ask questions. Listen for more than facts; listen for the emotions or feelings. Be careful. You may want to resolve the conflict quickly by stating policy or creating one.

Few conflicts are resolved simply by stating policy—just ask the supervisor working in customer service at your favorite store! If you have not listened carefully, you may assume that information will enlighten everyone and patch things up. Unfortunately, most conflicts are more complex than the basic facts, or the "he said" and "she said" parts of the conflict. Emotions and egos are often more central to the conflict than are facts.

Step 3:   If you have listened carefully for facts, emotions, and egos, then you can approach a resolution. You will have to balance the individual's needs with the ideal of being consistent. Fairness is more about consistency; it is about your side being heard and considered. Rules are guidelines; some are more flexible than others. Know the differences and understand that exceptions, when warranted, do not make you a weak leader. If you are not convinced, think about the disheartening media reports of school administrators using zero-tolerance policies without consideration for context.

Reflect:

1. What are some conflicts you have managed that would have been facilitated with a standard practice or policy?
2. What are some conflicts you have managed that were complicated by policy?
3. Do you know how to access your district's policy and practices?
4. What do you believe being *fair* means in regards to applying policy?

Remember, use policy

Policy can serve as a resource or a hindrance when managing conflict. Use policy as a tool to bring understanding and perhaps boundaries to a conflict.

23
Put Principles
Before Personalities

If you don't stand for something, you will fall for everything.
—Anonymous

Sometimes, keeping the focus on the problem and not the person is a real trick when managing conflict. I have found this to be almost impossible, as the person's personality will often be the balm that soothes the clash or the flame that fuels the concern. There is a saying in Alcoholics Anonymous: principles before personalities. This serves as a reminder that dealing with the facts of the conflict should take priority over the feelings we have for those involved.

Considering the relationships we have with others is essential in dealing with conflicts. Our goal should be to solve the conflict and preserve the relationship, despite our differences. On the other hand, there are conflicts where preserving the relationship is not as important to maintain (for instance, individuals we do not know well). In these situations, we often are more prone to force our position and get our way, at all costs.

When solving conflict with people we like, we are more likely to give in to preserve the relationship. Remember, solving conflicts is not about winning friends. Focus on solving problems while emphasizing principles and valuing people at the same time. Fairness, regardless of your like or dislike for a person, is essential.

Reflect:

1. Are you more likely to compromise with someone whom you like?

2. Think back to a recent conflict. How did the personalities affect the conflict and resolution?

Remember, put principles before personalities

Keep the focus on the problem and not on the person.

24
Listen With Empathy

One of the best ways to persuade others is with your ears—
by listening to them.
—Dean Rusk

Listening is a life skill, a leadership skill. The need to listen is sometimes so obvious that little time or training is given to develop the skill. However, just like typing at a computer or throwing a pass in football, listening can improve with information applied to practice.

Have you tried to talk to someone who would not listen? I have, and it can be frustrating. Recently, I was involved in a minor conflict with a stranger. We were waiting in a long line and as the line moved forward, she lost her place and assumed that I was trying to take her place in line. I was not; I just was not paying attention. She immediately jumped in front of me and claimed her place. I willingly agreed. I tried to explain but she interrupted me and responded, "Yea, whatever." I stepped back and bit my tongue. I allowed her to have the last word, as tempting as it was to respond.

In that situation, I disliked being interrupted, disregarded, not listened to, and not acknowledged. I offer this minor encounter as an example of when we do not listen. Have you recently ignored others or brushed them away? Actions speak louder than words. Listening communicates respect. When respect is absent, conflicts can escalate beyond the facts.

We cannot control if others listen to us, but we can improve our own listening behaviors. Others have described effective listening as active listening, reflective listening, and empathic listening. When you are an empathic listener, your main purpose is to let others express their thoughts and feelings. Initially, refrain from defending your position or thinking of your rebuttal. Instead, affirm what is said by nodding or saying "uh-huh." Occasionally, ask for more information without sounding interrogative. Think about your body language, give your attention, and focus to the person speaking. Do not give advice or discount their feelings by saying something such as, "It's not that bad." Be careful to not be critical or judge with either your words or your facial expressions. Being an empathic listener can diffuse many conflicts. Being an empathic listener builds trust and rapport. Listening with care is effective with adults and children.

People want to share their side of the story. Often, when others have their say and feel heard, you can then move forward with solving the conflict. Listening, like writing and speaking, is a skill. Listening communicates that you care, that the other person is important, and that you want to find a solution.

Reflect:

1. Think back to a time when others did not listen to you. How did it feel? What did you conclude?
2. Listening with empathy requires time. When is it worth the time to listen?

Remember, listen with empathy

Do not interrupt, interrogate, defend, give advice, or think about what you are going to say next while you are listening to someone talk.

25

Do Not Jump to Conclusions

Too many people confine their exercise to jumping to conclusions, running up bills, stretching the truth, bending over backward, lying down on the job, sidestepping responsibility and pushing their luck.
—Author Unknown

Leaders are defined by the decisions that they make. Leaders who base decisions on faulty assumptions and rumors accepted as fact will lose the respect and trust of followers. Attempts for improvement will be derailed and followers will comply but not commit.

We make conclusions every day. We have a need to make meaning and sense. We base our conclusions on our experiences and observations. We also base our conclusions on our assumptions. For example, a principal received his annual test scores and found that scores had declined in mathematics. Based on his past experience, he quickly concluded that the problem was the students' lack of basic math-fact mastery. He decided that all teachers would immediately begin to practice math facts every day for 10 minutes. He based his conclusion on the assumption that the practice would lead to higher scores. As you would imagine, simply practicing facts 10 minutes a day, without looking at the underlying problem more deeply, did not improve scores. Sometimes, our assumptions are correct; but assumptions can be a source of conflict and a basis for misunderstanding when they lead to hasty conclusions and actions.

Assumptions precede conclusions. When decisions are made in haste, criticism often follows. Why? Conclusions based on limited facts and untested assumptions tend to be unsound, unpopular, and even harmful. When we jump to a conclusion, we have few facts. We think we have enough facts and feel pressed to make a quick decision. Although there are times when leaders must make quick decisions, most decisions do not require such urgency.

The antidote to jumping to conclusions is patience. Pull back when you feel rushed and in need of a quick solution. Take some time to think, to examine your assumptions and your facts. How do you know they are true? Where might you find more information? Is a quick decision required? How can you involve others so that a good decision can be made?

Reflect:

1. Think back to a time that you jumped to conclusions and a resulting action. What facts guided your decision? Were the facts true?

2. How might others describe your decision-making skills?

3. What are some situations when a quick decision is necessary?

Remember, do not jump to conclusions

Leaders are defined by the decisions that they make.

26
Develop the Skills of Others

Practice is the best of all instructors.
—Publilius Syrus

Training can help us learn and refine skills that we may not have learned previously. Administrators have initiated programs to help students learn and practice conflict skills, such as conflict mediation programs. Just because we know the best way to handle conflict does not mean that we apply this with our own conflicts.

One strategy that can facilitate the conflict management skills of others is to provide ongoing practice opportunities. As a principal, I scheduled 15-minute segments at faculty meetings for developing conflict skills. I wanted faculty to have the skills to build high performing teams and to interact with a demanding community. At these practice sessions, reflection time was essential for faculty to analyze recent conflicts.

Suggestions that you may want to consider as you plan similar activities include:

1. Show that you accept conflict as normal. Express that you want to help others improve for reasons of their own personal growth and for the success of the school.

2. Use real situations with which your employees can relate. Provide a copy of scenarios for discussion and practice.

3. In the beginning, do not choose situations that involve extreme emotions or "hot topics" of your school. Be sensitive to employees who may feel criticized.

4. Use role-play groups (4-6) to help teachers analyze the various responses and reactions that individuals make to conflict.

5. Have teachers act out the five responses in the Introduction of this book and identify characteristics of each.
6. Discuss the benefits and disadvantages of each style.
7. Evaluate conflict resolution plans developed for students to find appropriate connections for adults.

As adults, we have witnessed conflicts on many occasions. We likely are responsible for teaching others how to resolve their differences and "fight fair." Even though we have the knowledge, we may be less skilled at applying strategies to our own conflicts. The wise leader will use the investment of development and training as a way to reduce future conflicts.

Reflect:

1. Generally, how would you rate your employees' abilities to manage conflict?
2. How frequently are conflicts at your school referred to you?
3. How can you allow for "practice" of handling conflict among your faculty?

Remember,

Allow time and provide real situations for employees to analyze and practice conflict management skills.

27
Be Sincere

If you would win a man to your cause,
first convince him that you are his sincere friend.
—Abraham Lincoln

I once had a principal who never wanted anyone mad at him. He told everyone what he or she wanted to hear, regardless of whether or not it was the truth. If I had a problem with a campus issue, he would agree with me on whatever solution I thought was best. However, when the next person came in with the same problem but a different solution, he agreed with that person too. We were *all* always right. That is what we like to hear, right? That we are always right—what better way to resolve a conflict? Wrong! At some point, we start to realize that we are not actually right, that perhaps our idea will not work, and that we were deprived of the chance to receive constructive and honest feedback on our idea in the first place. Most of us do not have to be right —what we want instead is to be heard; we want to receive an honest answer to our questions, even if the solution or answer is not what we had hoped for or wanted. An honest response is always better than one that is agreeable but hollow.

Be sincere with your answers, with everything you tell people. People figure out quickly when you only tell them what they want to hear; consequently, as soon as they are out the door, what you have said no longer means anything. They know that the next person will hear what he wants to hear, too, and that neither solution might actually happen. What a sinking feeling, to know that your principal does not care enough to be honest and sincere—that not running the risk of having to tell someone an answer that might make them unhappy is more important than being forthright. Your integrity is golden—be sure that what you say is what you mean, that your answers and responses in dealing with conflict are always honest and sincere.

Reflect:

1. Think about a time when a teacher came to you with a difficult question. Were you able to give her an honest answer, even if it was not what she wanted to hear?
2. How can you deliver unfavorable responses and consider others' feelings?
3. Is there ever a time when an honest, sincere answer is not the best approach?

Remember, be sincere

Sincerity is golden—it is one of the most valuable tools you can use in resolving conflict. Make sure your answers are honest, not hollow responses intended only to pacify a person who might get upset.

28

Communicate
With Your Superiors

No man is an island ...
—John Donne

I once had a parent who left my office furious, with a promise that she would be taking up her matter with someone more important and intelligent than me! I had disciplined her daughter for violating the dress code, and in doing so I had made decisions that were both fair and that complied completely with the school's dress code policy. Still, it was obvious to me that my supervisors would probably be hearing from this mother soon. I immediately called the assistant superintendent that I reported to and explained the entire situation to him in detail. He appreciated the advance notice of a problem that was likely coming his way, and I was able to tell my side of the story completely, without looking as though I had to defend my actions against a mother's cries of wrongdoing. Communicating with my supervisor offered a win-win situation and allowed us to resolve this potential conflict efficiently.

You do not have to be the judge and jury in every conflict situation; you do not have to be the only administrator involved, ready to tackle every issue all by yourself. In fact, in any major conflict situation, it is wise to let your supervisors know what is happening. If the conflict is not resolved to the satisfaction of one or both parties, there is always a chance that they might appeal the outcome to a higher level of authority. If that happens, you do not want an appeal to be the first time your supervisor has heard of the situation. Make sure that supervisors are informed, that they have a clear picture of all the facts, and that they know what your professional role in the situation was.

Meticulous documentation of major conflicts and all attempts and efforts made to resolve the conflict should also be maintained. The more serious the conflict or problem, the more precise the documentation should be. What might seem trivial to you could be a critical point to someone else. Unresolved conflict, particularly in certain circumstances (such as personnel issues, disciplinary decisions, or other potential "hotbeds") can lead to litigation, in which case you need as much accurate information as possible. You also want your supervisor's support in this matter, so be sure he or she is aware of the relevant facts of the situation. Not only does this keep communication and support lines open between you and your superiors, it also eliminates the possibility of surprises for your supervisor ... and most supervisors do not like surprises! Take some good advice from the people at Holiday Inn: "The best surprise is no surprise."

Reflect:

1. Do you have a system in place for documenting conflicts that arise on your campus?
2. Does this system include a means of notifying appropriate supervisors?
3. Reflect on conflicts on your campus. When did you choose not to notify your superiors? Why or why not?
4. In hindsight, was this the right decision? What circumstances would change the appropriateness of this decision?

Remember, communicate with your superiors

Make sure your superiors are aware of any issues that have potential consequences, particularly the potential for litigation. Develop and use a consistent method of documentation.

29
Be Patient and Take Your Time

A handful of patience is worth more than a bushel of brains.
— Dutch Proverb

Some people tend to be "thinkers," while others are "doers." Both personality types have important strengths that can be valuable for leaders, particularly when conflict arises. Those who are more action oriented like quick solutions and work to resolve a problem as soon as possible so that they can move on to tackle the next issue. In this sense, they accomplish a great deal of work and are highly motivated. Still, there are times when it pays to take your time and be patient with a conflict situation.

Being patient is often difficult for leaders, because leaders naturally want to solve problems and bring resolution to situations—it is part of the daily job. Being patient keeps you from saying things prematurely when you might not have all the information needed. When a phone call comes in at 5:30 on Friday afternoon, you may want to return the call or send an e-mail to resolve the problem before the weekend. Without the ability to contact people or gather additional information, this problem will simply have to wait until Monday. Thus, as a leader, you have to appreciate the value of patience, and allow yourself to become comfortable with being patient. In the words of historic statesman and inventor Benjamin Franklin, "He that can have patience can have what he will."

Reflect:

1. Have you ever rushed a solution or decision and then later realized that you should have taken more time?

2. What were the consequences of your impatience?

3. How can you distinguish between taking your time with a decision and being unresponsive?

4. Is taking your time with a decision the same as avoiding the conflict? Why or why not?

Remember, be patient and take your time

Do not rush important decisions. Like good soup, sometimes a conflict needs to simmer before it is ready to be resolved.

30
Look for a
Win-Win Solution

Sure, winning isn't everything. It's the only thing.
—Henry Sanders

No one wants to come out on the "losing" end of a situation. Losing implies defeat, that you were wrong, or that the other "side" was better than you were—these are difficult things to accept, and they typically lead to negative feelings. Thus, if you can find a way to resolve conflict with a win-win solution, then you can often leave the situation with everyone feeling positive. It also allows for more buy-in, or even acceptance and ownership, for the parties involved.

To work toward a win-win situation, you have to be willing to invest time. People need time to share their perspective and understand the other person's point of view. In addition, both parties have to be willing to seek a better solution, and willing to not get their way. It is your role as the leader to orchestrate this dialogue. Win-win involves synergy, where you take different entities and put them together to create something better—the whole is better than the sum of its parts.

As Vince Lombardi once said, "If winning isn't everything, why do they keep score?" Whether we keep score or not, everyone likes to win. And even more than they like to win, most people do not like to lose. Finding a win-win situation, then, empowers people and allows them to feel as though they have something to gain by resolving the conflict.

Reflect:

1. Think of a difficult conflict you have recently seen—was the solution a win-win approach? How did the outcome affect the parties involved?

2. What might be an example of a conflict in which a win-win solution is not possible? What do you as a leader do in those circumstances?

Remember, look for a win-win solution

Look for solutions where no one party has to completely give in.

31
Find
Common Ground

So, let us not be blind to our differences—
but let us also direct attention to our common interests
and to the means by which those differences can be resolved.
—John F. Kennedy

You become aware of a teacher not following the agreed-upon grading practices. The issue has been simmering and now is the time to address it. Before you meet with the teacher, think about the areas where you both agree. For example, you both have high standards for students and you both are student centered. You know that she is a good teacher. Let this common ground frame your discussion as you work toward solving the conflict.

Work to avoid any perception that you and the teacher are on opposite sides of the fence; the idea that you are on opposite sides implies that you have much farther to go to reach a solution. Instead, remind yourselves of the things that are important to both of you, including the fact that you are both committed to the learning and success of your students. If you can determine that you are actually both trying to achieve the same ultimate goal (student success), then resolving the conflict becomes a much easier, and definitely less stressful, task. Remember the words of Aesop, "United we stand, divided we fall."

Reflect:

1. How do you find common ground between two or more parties involved in a conflict?

2. In conflict situations among diverse groups, what sorts of things might be considered "common ground"?

3. Reflect on conflicts on your campus. When were you unable to find common ground for resolution?

4. What might you have done instead?

Remember, find common ground

Common ground gives everyone the same place to stand—equal footing.

Section III

Fine-Tuning Your Conflict Management Skills

By now you have a better understanding of conflict management. Along with the 17 strategies which improved your understanding, you have 14 additional strategies to help you be more proactive in managing conflict. This final section has 19 ideas to assist you in fine-tuning the conflict management skills that you are developing as a leader.

32
Examine Your Expectations

Shoot for the moon. Even if you miss, you'll land among the stars.
—Brian Littrell

Your expectations can be a source of conflict. As you reflect on a recent conflict, consider the role that expectations may have played.

For example, as a principal, I wanted to hire the very best teachers I could find. I wanted teachers to be obviously dedicated to the success of every student. Staff recruitment, selection, and retention were my highest priority. Consequently, I invested hours in reviewing applications, conducting interviews, and checking references. As a result, many of the teachers on the campus were highly committed to students and put in many extra hours beyond the "normal" workday. Campus administrators and mentor teachers coached and assisted the few teachers not meeting these expectations. The efforts resulted in a school filled with outstanding and dedicated teachers. High expectations became part of the fabric of the school.

As the district grew, patterns of campus enrollments changed. Some campuses grew quickly; others experienced declining student enrollments. As a result, district administrators reassigned teachers to schools with openings.

If you have been a principal in such a situation, you can predict the conflicts. Teachers were reassigned with minimal input from the principals. In several cases, teachers who needed a change thrived in a new setting. Yet, I often received the teachers in need of a "change" who had been hired by another principal. When this happened, I inquired and was told that the fair way to reassign teachers was to distribute the concerns and allow these teachers another chance. After all, we had a great campus!

I understand that some teachers need a fresh start, but I did not think this was fair. It seemed that our school was being "rewarded" with more challenges.

Regardless of whether you agree or disagree about the fairness of the situation, balancing your expectations can help you manage conflict.

In the end, I accepted the decision and welcomed the teachers (after I shared my thoughts with the district administrators). I was wrong about some of the teachers; they really did thrive. Yet, with others, we offered assistance and eventually helped some decide that they had better options than teaching.

You may experience conflict when you feel disappointed or frustrated and your expectations are not met. Researchers have connected high expectations to increased student achievement. It is not wrong to have expectations and goals. Recognize when unmet expectations are at the heart of a conflict. You can then examine the expectations and decide if they were reasonable or even possible. Having a building of dedicated teachers is a worthy goal; every child deserves such a teacher. However, to expect perfection in the midst of district growth is not always possible. Shoot for the stars and learn to be "okay" when you land on the moon instead.

Reflect:

1. How would you describe your expectations related to your performance?
2. How would you describe the expectations of teachers and students?
3. Consider a recent conflict. What were your expectations related to the incident?
4. How can the act of identifying the expectations (yours and others) help you manage future conflicts?

Remember, examine your expectations

Shoot for the stars; be willing to accept it when you land on the moon instead.

જ્જ્જ્

33
Know When Your Standards Are Too High

The nice thing about standards is that
there are so many of them to choose from.
—Andrew S. Tanenbaum

I have high standards and a little bit of pride when I claim that! Do you have high standards? Do your coworkers, your spouse, or your children frequently disappoint you? Are the standards for you and others reasonable, given the time, energy, and resources available? Conflicts can occur when our standards are unreasonable or when we have not clearly communicated our standards.

Recently, we coordinated a large conference. We invested many hours of planning, arranging room reservations, refreshments, and audiovisual equipment. We produced slick flyers and many participants registered. We arranged several guest speakers and planned a schedule of sessions. The program was prepared and three people carefully edited every word; yet at the conference, we found several mistakes in the program. Ugh!

One of my challenges involves keeping my standards in check. I wanted an error-free publication; it was about 98% error free. Considering the available staff and time, this was our best possible effort. It is likely that some noticed the mistakes, but the mistakes did not affect the outcomes of the conference for those attending. Sometimes, high standards can lead us into conflict.

For those of you with perfectionist tendencies, it may sound like heresy to "lower" your standards. In reality, rather than lowering standards, you might learn to select the most important ones. Having high standards does not mean being inflexible; instead, by keeping the focus on what is important, we avoid situations that instigate conflict.

One way to manage your standards is to extend the same measure of grace and kindness that you would like extended to you. There are times in our lives when we cannot maintain our own standards or those of others. Illness. Divorce. Debt. Emergencies. Babies. Aging parents. Life happens for me, you, and teachers, too. Offer help, compassion, understanding, and time. You will do well to make adjustments.

Reflect:

1. As a leader of the school, what are your standards for yourself?

2. How do you manage the frustration and disappointment of not meeting goals that you or your school has established?

3. Do you believe that you must do everything well or, if you do not, then you are incompetent?

Remember, know when your standards are too high

By keeping the focus on what is important, we avoid situations that create conflict for our families and coworkers.

34
Invite Difference

Honest differences are often a healthy sign of progress.
—Mahatma Ghandi

One source of conflict tends to happen when we interact with people who are different than we are. We tend to be most comfortable with people who are like us in dress, appearance, and tastes. We find conversation and relating to be easier when we have things in common.

Some of us may lack knowledge about different groups and cultures, as we may have had little chance for interaction. Because we lack understanding, we tend to assume that others have experienced the world in the same way we have.

Each culture has specific beliefs, foods, customs, holidays, religious beliefs, and celebrations. Some have different languages. Although there are obvious differences between various ethnic and cultural groups, many times there are more differences among the individuals within the same group.

In addition, there are many other types of groups besides those based on culture. We may mentally group students in our schools by where they live, whether they rent or own a home, and by the characteristics of their parents (volunteers, working moms, college educated, etc.). What are some of the subgroups in your school--ethnic, economic, geographic, and others?

Do you have a tendency to generalize or make assumptions? As principal of an ethnically diverse student body, I interacted with parents from various ethnic groups. After a few months, I noticed that a few fathers from one cultural group would not shake my hand but would greet the assistant principal, who was a man. I thought their actions were disrespectful and due to me being a woman. I felt offended, but kept quiet. It was not until I learned more about the norms of specific cultures that I realized that these fathers were actually treating me with respect. Because we lack understanding, we sometimes make untrue assumptions. Untested assumptions can add fuel to future fires.

When we invite opportunities to learn and interact with those different from us, we widen our perspectives. Such openness and understanding can serve as a resource in times of conflict.

Reflect:

1. Recently, what have you learned about others' differences?
2. When was the last time you experienced a new culture, food, or event?
3. What are some of the assumptions you have about different demographic groups of students in your school?
4. How have you increased the understanding of various groups?

Remember, invite difference

When we invite opportunities to learn and interact with those who may be different from us, we widen our perspectives.

35
Look Below the Surface

There is more than meets the eye.
You will never know all the facts.
—Anonymous

Sometimes you might find yourself immersed in a conflict where you do not have all the information and you do not know the history. For example, once I found myself in the middle of a conflict between veteran teachers. The teachers did not agree on how to spend their team's limited budget money. The conflict escalated quickly and lasted for weeks. They involved other staff members and sides were forming. I answered questions about the budget and soon found my words taken out of context. Personal attacks ensued. I found it odd that the conflict was so intense and personal about what I thought was a simple issue. After some investigating, I learned that these two teachers had many unresolved differences from the past. Their conflict was about power, turf wars, and gaining supporters rather than a simple fight over money. After learning more of the facts, I was able to serve as a more effective facilitator and address some of the underlying issues.

When you experience conflict where individuals are expressing intense emotions, look beneath the surface. Recognize the role of unresolved issues. Understand that you do not have all the relevant facts. Step away. Say as little as possible. Gather more information. Trust your instincts. The truth is probably somewhere in the middle. Paul Harvey, radio personality and the voice behind *The Rest of the Story*, shared the multiple sides to an issue in the news, ending with the catch phrase "And now you know the rest of the story." Remember, there is likely a "rest of the story" which you will need to learn to effectively manage some conflicts.

Reflect:

1. When was the last time you experienced or witnessed a conflict with individuals who had a history of past conflicts?
2. How were these conflicts different from those without a history?
3. Think about a conflict you have witnessed where individuals expressed intense emotions. What might have been underlying factors in the conflict?

Remember, look below the surface

Recognize the role of unresolved issues. Understand when you do not have all the relevant facts.

36
Consider That Timing Is Everything

Sometimes being a friend means mastering the art of timing.
There is a time for silence. A time to let go ...
And a time to prepare to pick up the pieces when it's all over.
—Gloria Naylor

Timing is everything in investments, politics, treating an illness, asking for a raise, and running a race. Timing is everything, too, when managing conflicts.

Consider the timing of your response in a conflict. Are you quick to provide an answer? Do you act in haste? Unless the situation is an emergency, we suggest that you acknowledge the situation and promise to get back with others involved. By allowing individuals time to cool down and to collect their thoughts, you can face the conflict with greater objectivity. Resist the temptation to provide a directive, either verbally or in an e-mail. We have witnessed the use of e-mail in conflict situations and have found that such responses sometimes create more conflicts than they resolve.

Consider timing when you are planning to address a concern that could develop into conflict. As a principal, you will have many opportunities to address personnel concerns. You will consider the importance of each situation, using wisdom to let some things go and using courage to address situations of concern. When you need to schedule a conference with employees, consider the other events happening in their lives, balanced with the nature of the concern. For example, you have scheduled a meeting with a teacher to address concerns related to her recent lesson. A few days before the meeting, the court serves the teacher with papers for a divorce. It would be wise to consider timing and reschedule the conference for a future date, unless you observed issues related to student safety or welfare that must be addressed immediately. As leaders, we show our concern and support when we treat others with the same consideration and kindness that we would appreciate in similar situations.

A leader is sensitive to timing. When you have built relationships and trust with others, you will be more aware of the issues that affect timing.

Reflect:

1. Think back to a time that a supervisor discussed her concerns with you. Were there other events that influenced your ability to hear and understand the concerns?

2. To what degree are you aware of events and challenges in the professional and/or personal lives of your employees? How can you get this kind of information?

3. How might knowing your employees as people help you understand timing when managing conflicts?

Remember, consider that timing is everything

Understand the importance of timing. Balance patience with action when managing conflict.

37
Be a Role Model

Be the change you wish to see in the world.
—Mahatma Ghandi

What you model is what you get. How you want teachers and students to handle conflict will be determined by how they see you handle conflict.

When you became an administrator, you probably understood the feeling that E.F. Hutton had—"when E.F. Hutton talks, people listen." E.F. Hutton was a brokerage firm best known for its commercials in the 1980s. The commercials typically involved individuals remarking in a crowded room that their broker was E.F. Hutton, which caused all noise to cease. Yes, there are times when all eyes are on you, particularly in times of conflict.

Others will observe your interactions with parents during conflict. Teachers will hear about your actions with other teachers through the grapevine. Students will observe your actions and words during discipline conferences. Do you yell, belittle, and criticize? Do you listen? Do you give orders and directives? Do you let others share their side of the story? Do you talk to students differently than you talk to adults? On the other hand, do you smile and find the nearest exit? Do you lack courage to face the conflicts? Are you labeled as a leader who does not like conflict and will not do anything?

More than what you say, others will do what you do. If you are committed to developing your skills in conflict management, others will be more likely to follow, either out of a desire to please you or because you have helped them see how such skills are helpful. As you model the conflict skills that you would like others to use, you will help develop teams that respond to conflict and ultimately use the conflict as one tool for improvement.

Reflect:

1. How do you respond when someone questions your integrity, character, or intelligence?
2. How do your actions in student-discipline situations measure up to the skills that will help them with conflict as adults?
3. How do you deal with frustration and anger?
4. What do you think the teachers would say about your approaches to conflict management?
5. If you were a teacher, would you consider someone like yourself a role model, particularly when managing conflict?

Remember, be a role model

What you model is what you will get.

38
Consider the Relationship

The ultimate test of a relationship is to disagree but hold hands.
—Alexander Penney

The relationship is an essential consideration when dealing with conflict. Conflicts vary by their content and the nature of the relationships between those involved. One prevention strategy for conflicts is to invest time in developing relationships with those with whom you interact.

Think about a conflict that happened with a close friend. If you faced the conflict, the relationship was likely tested. Strengths or weaknesses of the relationship were revealed. Sometimes we have commented, "She really wasn't my friend after all." When we trust someone, we often extend more grace and forgiveness than we would with strangers. As a result, we may let situations build to a boiling point and find we have a conflict with multiple layers. The relationship will serve as a resource or a hindrance in resolving such conflicts.

Besides strangers, we interact with many people with whom we work but do not know well. When there is no relationship, we may be less tolerant and more critical. We do not understand their point of view. We may not see them as individuals, like ourselves, who have strengths and challenges. Conflicts may be more frequent with acquaintances than with friends.

Leaders who understand the importance of relationships take the time to learn about others. They allow time for faculty to interact professionally as well as personally. They make a point to greet the students and their parents. They encourage teachers to interact with parents early in the school year and to establish rapport with students. They assist new faculty and students by providing orientation activities and opportunities to meet others. Leaders who value relationships encourage teams to work together and play together.

Reflect:

1. Think about a conflict you have had with a friend. How did you handle the situation? Are you still friends?

2. Think about a conflict involving a parent or teacher who was also a good personal friend. How did your relationship interact with the situation? What was difficult about the conflict as compared to other situations?

3. Think about a time that you complained to a customer service representative (bank, credit card, store). Would you have acted differently if you learned that the representative was a friend or acquaintance?

Remember, consider the relationship

Understand that the relationship is an essential consideration when dealing with conflict.

39
Master the
Art of Apology

Oh, it seems to me that sorry seems to be the hardest word.
—Elton John

We all know that "to err is human, but to forgive is divine" (Alexander Pope). But what about apologizing—is that human or divine, or somewhere in between? Sometimes a simple apology can work wonders for resolving conflict or repairing a relationship that has been damaged by conflict. In one school, a teacher was hurt by a coworker's lapse in professional judgment. The teacher had worked with her coworker on a curriculum writing project, and they both had contributed a great deal of time and energy to developing teaching strategies. Several weeks later, the teacher saw that her colleague had published the ideas in a well-known publication for classroom teachers. The teacher's name was nowhere to be seen on the article—it was as if she had never contributed to the project at all. In fact, she had not even known that the piece had been submitted. After talking to her principal, the teacher finally approached her colleague and explained how she was surprised and confused by what had happened. While expecting a series of excuses as to why the teacher's name was not included on the publication, the teacher's questions were answered with a simple, "I'm sorry—I was wrong, I should not have done this, and I apologize." The teacher was surprised, yet amazed at how this simple but honest response impacted her.

What was done was done—the article could not be retracted, nor could they go back and pretend it had not happened. Still, the apology from her colleague allowed the teacher to know that her feelings were validated and that the colleague wanted to repair the relationship and move forward without trying to justify her error in judgment. As simple as it sounds, a sincere apology works.

Reflect:

1. When was the last time you apologized for the role you played in a conflict? Was the apology sincere?
2. Did the apology have an impact on resolving the conflict or on the other person's perception of what happened?
3. How do you react when someone apologizes to you, particularly when you are involved in conflict with that person?
4. When might an apology not be an effective approach to handling conflict?

Remember, master the art of apology

Never be afraid to say "I'm sorry." There is nothing weak in making such a statement. Be gracious in receiving an apology as well as giving one.

40
Admit Your Mistakes

Always acknowledge a fault.
This will throw those in authority off their guard
and give you an opportunity to commit more.
—Mark Twain

Recently I had a brief but heated argument with a colleague at work. My feelings had been hurt about her lack of communication on something I had considered to be important, so I snapped at her about it and a conflict ensued. After some strong words, I realized how silly and meaningless the conflict had been. Sure, it would have been nice if she had kept me "in the loop," but in truth the issue was not a big deal and really had no impact on me anyway. I immediately stopped and apologized, saying that I should not have snapped at her over such a trivial matter. To my surprise, she apologized as well. By simply admitting that I had been wrong, the conflict was defused almost immediately and we could both move on and still feel comfortable about our relationship.

As with offering an apology, admitting your mistakes is a big first step in resolving conflict. Conflict is similar to communication in that it requires two people—it is a two-way street and requires the interaction of both parties for anything to take place. With that in mind, in many cases the conflict arises from issues that have taken place on both sides of this two-way street. Rarely are there simply a victim and a perpetrator; more typical is a situation where both parties have pushed a little hard, dug in their heels, or failed to communicate effectively with others. Thus, there is usually a good opportunity to admit your role in the conflict, even if you think the other person is "more" at fault. Acknowledge whatever part you might have played, however small that part might be. This allows the other person to feel less defensive and to know that a positive outcome can be reached without one side having to be entirely to blame. Blame is heavy—it is a much lighter burden when it is shared on more than one set of shoulders, and it allows for compromise and apology to come more easily.

Reflect:

1. How difficult is it for you to readily recognize and admit your mistakes?
2. Reflect on a recent conflict in which you were involved—what role did you play in the conflict?
3. What strategies might you use to help someone else acknowledge his or her role in a conflict?
4. What do you do when a person flatly refuses to acknowledge her role in a conflict?
5. Are there other ways to reach resolution?

Remember, admit your mistakes

Mistakes are not bad—they are opportunities for improvement. Recognizing your role in a conflict, however big or small, is a critical step toward resolution.

41
Use the
Healing Power of Humor

A laugh is a mighty good thing,
and rather too scarce a good thing.
—Herman Melville

It was 3 days before Thanksgiving. A man had a parrot who swore a lot. One day he told the parrot, "If you swear again, I am going to put you in the freezer." So the parrot promised he wouldn't swear. A minute later he swore. The man said, "You have to stop, or I'm really going to put you in the freezer." Again the parrot promised he wouldn't swear. But later, he swore again; the man grabbed the parrot and stuffed him in the freezer. The next day, he took the parrot out of the freezer. Shivering, the parrot said, "Wh-wh-what did the turkey do?"

Have you ever known one of those people who can make you smile even when you are really upset? Research has shown that humor is actually good for your health. On a recent Oprah Winfrey television segment, Dr. Tracy Gaudet (2007) explained that researchers have found that laughter helps your immune system fight invading viruses and cancers. Humor lowers levels of the stress hormone cortisol and can lower your blood pressure and decrease heart strain. Bill Cosby, while best known as a hugely successful comedian, also endured great tragedy when his only son was killed in a car jacking; still, Cosby believes in the power of humor: "Through humor, you can soften some of the worst blows that life delivers. And once you find laughter, no matter how painful your situation might be, you can survive it." In the words of Erma Bombeck, "If you can't make it better, you can laugh at it."

Reflect:

1. To the extent possible and appropriate, have you used humor in dealing with conflict on your campus?

2. What impact have you seen humor have on situations involving conflict?

3. What can you do to inject humor into a situation appropriately?

4. In what situations might humor be completely inappropriate?

Remember, use the healing power of humor

Whenever possible and appropriate, make people smile. Maintain a friendly and positive disposition when dealing with conflict.

42
Do Not
Overreact

It has been said that man is a rational animal.
All my life I've been searching for evidence that could support this.
—Bertrand Russell

In response to another district's adoption of a highly innovative technology program, our curriculum director decided that next year we would equip every student in one of our large high schools with a laptop computer and would require teachers to use technology in all facets of instruction. As we sat in a meeting discussing this, I asked some questions about how this would be accomplished and if we had considered the problems that might arise. Later, the curriculum director pulled me aside and told me that she felt I was being disloyal to her for raising these questions in front of a committee. In reality, my questions were sincere—I raised them because I felt they were legitimate concerns that we needed to consider. It had nothing to do with my loyalty to the curriculum director. I believe she overreacted. Her statements surprised me and I wondered if she was taking any type of questioning as a personal attack.

Emotion can often take over, replacing rational thinking. And when you are not thinking rationally, it is often hard to make reasonable decisions. Thus, being rational and reasonable are critical components to effectively resolving conflict. When you overreact to a conflict or problem, the focus can shift from the problem to your reaction. An unreasonable reaction can also cause you to lose credibility. People are watching and they expect you, as the leader, to be reasonable in your reactions. Overreacting may even harm relationships, destroying trust between you and others. Rebuilding this trust is a difficult and time-consuming process. Many (if not most) situations require that you have some sort of reaction. Just be careful that your reaction is not an overreaction. Your role as the leader is to solve and facilitate conflict, not to add to it or make it worse.

Reflect:

1. What does it mean to be reasonable and rational in dealing with conflict?

2. Can you think of a time when you were not reasonable or rational as you dealt with conflict? What were the circumstances? The outcome?

3. What might you do differently in the future?

Remember, do not overreact

Avoid making judgments based primarily on emotion.

43
Change Behaviors, Not People

The more things change, the more they remain … insane.
—from *Over the Hedge,* movie by Dreamworks Animation
(created by Michael Fry & T. Lewis)

It is next to impossible to change people—just ask any couple who has been married for more than a few months! What is much more possible to change, however, is behavior. In a conflict situation, you must focus on changing the behavior that has caused conflict, not the person.

I used to have a teacher on my campus who was not a good communicator. She called impromptu practices and meetings and was generally ineffective at communicating both with students and especially with parents. Still, she was an outstanding, gifted theater teacher and very dedicated to her job, and I could see that she had the potential for great success. What she needed was improvement in some of her actions regarding communication.

Recognizing both the teacher's talents and deficiencies, I worked with the teacher to set parameters to help her be more effective. She agreed to schedule all practices at least a week in advance. She submitted detailed lesson plans and then followed them. She began to communicate with parents, by phone and in writing, on a regular basis. These sorts of parameters provided the structure that the teacher needed to operate efficiently, without focusing on her weaknesses. I could not change the teacher, and trying to do so would have been frustrating and ineffective. Instead, I worked with her to identify and alter her problem behaviors; by focusing on these behaviors and not on the teacher herself, I could help her change her behavior without causing her to feel personally attacked.

Comedian Carol Burnett once said, "Only I can change my life. No one can do it for me." You cannot change people, but you can help them change their behavior. If behaviors are a source of conflict, then focusing on how to effectively change these behaviors is a critical step toward resolution.

Reflect:

1. Think about someone that you wish would change their behaviors. What are the behaviors?

2. How can you separate the behaviors from the person's personal characteristics?

3. How can you effectively work to change specific behaviors in yourself?

Remember, change behaviors, not people

Separate personality from behavior—one can change, the other cannot.

44
Think Creatively–
Step Outside That Box

Change is the law of life.
And those who look only to the past or present
are certain to miss the future.
—John F. Kennedy

A common phrase in recent years has been to think outside the box. Exactly what is the box? If we knew the answer to that, handling conflict would be much easier! However, what can be helpful in dealing with conflict is an approach that allows you to think creatively—to imagine a solution that might be a little different from what one would traditionally consider.

Consider the story of a woman who cooked her pot roast from a family recipe, one that had been passed down from generation to generation. Based on the family tradition, she always cut each end off the roast before cooking it. One day, her daughter asked her why she cut off the ends—did it make the roast taste better, did it allow for faster cooking, what "special" reason was there for cutting off the ends? "I don't know," her mother replied. Even her mother's mother did not know—"that's just how we do it." Eventually, when they asked her mother's grandmother, a 98-year old family matriarch, they learned the reason. "My roasting pan was too small for the roast. I had to cut off the ends to make it fit." Thus, they had cut the ends of their roast for three generations, not knowing that it added absolutely no value to the recipe. This same lesson applies to conflict situations as well.

Sometimes we do things a certain way just because it is the way it has always been done; there is really not a good reason. As a leader, step outside the box and find a better way. Think of the opportunities that are lost when people refuse to try a new way of doing things:

Two roads diverged in a wood, and I—
I took the one less traveled by,
And that has made all the difference.

—Robert Frost (1874-1963), "The Road Not Taken"

Reflect:

1. Think about a conflict that recently occurred on your campus—did you consider any solutions that might be considered nontraditional?
2. What might alternative decisions have looked like?
3. In what situations is a creative approach not appropriate?
4. What are the advantages and disadvantages of handling a conflict situation creatively?

Remember, think creatively—step outside that box

Consider approaches that you might not have used before. Listen to new viewpoints and ideas.

45
Explore
Multiple Options

Don't fear failure so much that you refuse to try new things.
The saddest summary of a Life contains three descriptions:
could have, might have, and should have.
— Louis E. Boone

Do you know the old saying that two heads are better than one? As a leader, whenever there is a problem, people look to you for guidance. Obviously, you do not have all the answers, but it is up to you to establish the climate where people feel free to share their opinions, good or bad. One way to do this is to use good brainstorming strategies. Brainstorming does not just allow people to share their ideas, but it allows them to share these ideas without fear of being ridiculed or belittled.

You have to build trust and develop a climate where people feel that their ideas are respected and valued to facilitate brainstorming. Using this strategy, everyone has a right to an opinion. No one should love their own ideas to the degree that they are not open to the ideas of others. No opinion or person should be made to look foolish. The goal of brainstorming is to generate as many ideas as possible. These ideas are not evaluated during the idea generation stage—no criticism is allowed, as this may cause people to feel uncomfortable in thinking and sharing more ideas. Other ways to explore multiple options include contacting other people, visiting schools, and searching the literature for more information on the topic. Mark Twain recognized the value of exploring multiple options when he said, "I don't give a damn for a man that can only spell a word one way."

Reflect:

1. Are you in love with your ideas? Or are you open to multiple options?
2. Do people feel that they can openly share new ideas with you?
3. What do you do to nurture new ideas on your campus?
4. How can you use the strategy of brainstorming to facilitate the management of conflict?

Remember, explore multiple options

Look at as many options as possible so that you can find the solution that best fits the needs of all parties involved.

46
Think
Long Term

Don't mistake a bump in the road for the horizon.
— Joel Barker

There once was a fisherman from a small village who, as he made his way to the river to do his fishing for the day, noticed something floating in the water. As he got closer, he realized that what he saw was a baby. He jumped in, grabbed the baby, and carried it to the bank of the river. Then he noticed more babies floating down the river. Immediately he realized that he needed to see what was causing this to happen. The fisherman ran upstream and saw a large ogre standing in the middle of the river, putting babies on banana leaves and pushing them downstream. The ogre saw him and complained that he was bored and had nothing better to do. The fisherman invited the ogre back to the village, where he could help the villagers. The ogre was happy to have something to do and to feel valued; the village had a new worker, bigger and stronger than any of the villagers, and no more babies went floating down the river.

The moral of this story is that thinking long term (heading upstream to find the cause of the problem) led to a way to solve the conflict. While short-term solutions can often be good Band-Aids, they typically do not get to the root of a problem. For example, when making decisions about using a new curriculum or implementing a new dress code policy, think beyond what might happen right now. What impact will this have next year, or in 2 years, or even 5 or more years from now? Thinking long term works toward a solution that will prevent unanticipated conflict and often leads to an investment that reaps benefits for all. Prevention, rather than intervention, is always a more effective approach. The old saying that an ounce of prevention is worth a pound of cure holds true for schools, as well. Think about what potential pitfalls there might be with any decision you make. It can save you much time and effort in the long run, rather than later having to "fix" issues that should have been foreseen.

Reflect:

1. Based on a recent conflict you experienced, what are the long-term consequences of the situation?
2. How did the resolution of this conflict affect the long-term implications?
3. If you see that long-term consequences are problematic, what can you do?

Remember, think long term

Prevention, rather than intervention, is always a more effective approach.

47
Keep it Simple

The main thing is to keep the main thing the main thing.
—Stephen Covey

When I was principal, every year we had an annual carnival sponsored by the PTA. Our purpose was to build community with this event. However, every year the carnival planning became more and more complicated, resulting in a number of raging conflicts, such as different groups arguing over who would do what, how profits would be more fairly distributed, and spent. My role was to remind everyone of the purpose of the event—building community. When you become embroiled in a conflict such as this, take all the facts and place them under the umbrella of the event's purpose. Then, reduce these elements to that simple focus. Remember the goal of the event. Do not let the complexity of the conflict overshadow the purpose of the activity. Remind yourself to focus on an important question: why are we doing this?

I am reminded of a story about someone trying to name the Seven Wonders of the World. The individual thought and thought but could not name them all. A child was asked the same question and quickly responded: to see, to hear, to touch, to taste, to feel, to laugh, and to love. Of course, these wonders are even more spectacular than the Grand Canyon or the Taj Mahal. Sometimes we forget to keep the main thing the main thing.

Reflect:

1. Have you done everything you can to keep a conflict resolution process simple?

2. What sorts of superfluous issues might make this difficult?

3. How do you determine what is important to an issue and what is not important?

Remember, keep it simple

The simple way is almost always the best way. Never make something harder than it has to be.

48
Know Your
Limits

Take rest; a field that has rested gives a bountiful crop.
—Ovid

Do you know how to cook a frog? Put a frog in a large pot of warm water on a cold stove; frogs like water. Slowly adjust the flame, increasing the heat every 5 minutes. The frog will enjoy the warmth, but by the time he feels the heat, he is unable to escape. He is without defense. Does your job feel as if you are jumping from one hot pot to another?

Dealing with conflicts on a regular basis places you at risk of burnout. In the heat of your work, you may be unaware that prolonged fatigue, which IS not relieved by rest, and a detachment from your work are signs of burnout. Burnout is different from stress. Although the symptoms such as irritability, anger, fatigue, and anxiety may be similar, stress can be relieved by rest and relaxation.

Researchers Brock and Grady (2002) have found that exhaustion can occur because of stressful interpersonal contacts common in the daily work of school leaders. The constant and prolonged interaction can be draining. How many times a day do you hear "Got a minute?" Indeed, the job is stressful. What can you do?

Consider the strategies presented in this book. How well do you recognize and accept your limits and those of others? Do not let pride or fear prevent you from setting limits. How well do you take care of yourself? Prevent burnout. Good nutrition, rest, and exercise are essential. Do you take regular breaks during the day, week, and year? Change your routine. Take a walk around your school. Schedule an occasional afternoon off. Get some fresh air, sunshine, and perspective.

Reflect:

1. How would you describe the frequency and intensity of the conflicts you face at work?
2. How often do you feel irritability, anger, fatigue, anxiety, or apathy?
3. What are your strategies for renewal?

Remember, know your limit

Change your routine. Take a walk around your school. Schedule an occasional afternoon off. Get some fresh air, sunshine, and perspective.

49

Do Not
Blame Everyone

*Few things help an individual more
than to place responsibility upon him,
and to let him know that you trust him.*
— Booker T. Washington

Have you ever received one of those memos addressed to the entire staff, when really the issue concerns just one or two people who are engaging in a problematic or unacceptable behavior? Don't you hate that? Some faculty members feel as though they have been scolded, when a simple face-to-face conversation with the parties who are involved would have solved the matter without drawing undue attention to it or without potentially alienating or hurting the feelings of people who know nothing of it.

One time our entire faculty received a memo in our mailboxes telling us to watch what we said at school ball games. Apparently, there had been a complaint that two teachers attending a school soccer game had used inappropriate language; parents had heard the teachers' conversation and complained to the principal. Rather than address the problem with the two teachers involved in the complaint, the principal chose to put a memo in everyone's box. All teachers who had attended the soccer game then worried about what they had said at the game—had they said something inappropriate? If so, what was it? An entire group of teachers who had nothing to do with the situation and who had done nothing wrong worried, wondering if they were being addressed in the memo. Meanwhile, the people to whom the reprimand was actually addressed likely did not even recognize their error. Thus, the memo was ineffective at two levels: it caused undue worry to undeserving faculty, and it failed to address the inappropriate behavior with the people who needed it. The lesson here—make sure you have the courage to address issues with the people who have acted inappropriately; do not blame everyone or resort to group reminders about specific instances. Save mass memos for issues that are informative for everyone. Specific and individual behaviors should be addressed in just that manner—specifically and on an individual basis. And by all means, refrain from the urge to send a quick e-mail to address conflict with individuals.

Reflect:

1. Have you ever received one of those memos that seem to chastise everyone for an individual's behavior? How did that make you feel? Why might a leader handle situations in this way?

2. How can you address inappropriate behavior with teachers?

3. When might it be appropriate to address behavior with a larger group?

Remember, do not blame everyone

Address inappropriate behaviors with the people who engaged in them; do not address the behavior with people who had nothing to do with it.

50
Embrace Conflict

Difficulties are meant to rouse, not discourage.
The human spirit is to grow strong by conflict.
—William Ellery Channing

Conflict is a learning experience. It is temporary. It should always present an opportunity for personal growth. With these ideas in mind, embrace conflict. Consider the possibilities that a conflict situation presents. Can you help change a negative into a positive-- perhaps something that will result in improvements on your campus? Conflict brings opportunity, and opportunity should never be wasted. Find the positive, the growth opportunity, in almost every conflict that you face as a leader. Keep a journal about how you have handled conflict and what positive things resulted from the situation. This will help you learn not to fear conflict, and especially not to dread it, but to face conflict as a chance to really make a difference. What a fantastic prospect!

Reflect:

1. Think of a time when you were scared of a conflict. How did things turn out? Were your fears unfounded?
2. Did you grow from the experience?
3. How can you learn from this experience and apply it to future conflict situations?
4. How can you embrace conflict?

Remember, embrace conflict

Conflict is healthy, it is natural, and it is temporary. View conflict as a positive learning experience.

෨෨෨

Conclusion

*Peace is not the absence of conflict but the presence of
creative alternatives for responding to conflict ...*
—Dorothy Thompson

As we noted earlier, leaders live in a world of conflict. It is just the
nature of the job. However, we are not alone in our efforts to manage conflict. As Lyndon B. Johnson said, "There are no problems we
cannot solve together, and very few we can solve by ourselves."
Because conflict management is as much about working with others
as it is about actually solving issues, the ability to manage conflict
successfully can make the difference between being a leader and
being a good leader. The following is a list of 10 important reminders
that should guide your actions when responding to conflict.

The 10 Reminders

- **I Reaffirm** the belief that conflict has value
- **I Recognize** the problem AS a problem
- **I Resolve** to be involved in positive solutions
- **I Respond** in a timely manner
- **I Reflect** on possible solutions
- **I Review** as much information as possible
- **I Rely** on trustworthy sources
- **I Repair** relationships that are broken
- **I Restore** trust to the organization
- **I Reinforce** continual improvement

In the Appendix you will find a checklist of the 10 reminders that can be used to rate how you respond to conflict when you use the conflict management strategies in this book. We suggest that you do this at several intervals throughout the year to evaluate your improvement. When you frame your responses to conflict within these 10 reminders, you will find that your actions are purposeful and focused on reducing conflict. Better yet, the conflict management strategies that you develop and implement will lead to preventing conflict later. In this way, you will spend less time "running for cover" and more time being an effective leader building a stronger school.

Appendix

The 10 Reminders

Consider the conflict management strategies that you use throughout the day on your campus. Do you frame your responses using the 10 reminders below? Assess yourself to see just how well you are doing.

1–Never   2–Rarely   3–Sometimes   4–Usually   5–Always

1. **I Reaffirm** the belief that conflict has value   _____

2. **I Recognize** the problem AS a problem   _____

3. **I Resolve** to be involved in positive solutions   _____

4. **I Respond** in a timely manner   _____

5. **I Reflect** on possible solutions   _____

6. **I Review** as much information as possible   _____

7. **I Rely** on trustworthy sources   _____

8. **I Repair** relationships that are broken   _____

9. **I Restore** trust to the organization   _____

10. **I Reinforce** continual improvement   _____

Total Score   _____

Score Results:
50-45 - You are a GREAT conflict manger
44-40 - You are a GOOD conflict manager
39-35 - You are ALMOST a good conflict manager
34-30 - You need help in becoming a better conflict manager
29-25 - You need a vacation!

In the next grading period, evaluate yourself again—see if you are remembering to frame your responses to conflict using conflict management strategies effectively.

References

Anderson, M. J. (2007). Principals and conflict management: Do preparation programs do enough? *AASA Journal of Scholarship and Practice, 4*(1), 4-13.

Bagin, D., & Gallagher, D. (2001). *The school and community relations* (7th ed.). Boston: Allyn & Bacon.

Barnett, D. (2004). The dark side of school leadership: Implications for administrator preparation. *Leadership and Policy in Schools, 3*(4), 245.

Brock, B. L., & Grady, M. L. (2002). *Avoiding burnout: A principal's guide to keeping the fire alive.* Thousand Oaks, CA: Corwin Press.

Covey, S. M. R. (2006). *The speed of trust: The one thing that changes Everything.* New York: Free Press.

Enemark, D. (2006). It's all about me: Why e-mails are so easily misunderstood. *The Christian Science Monitor* [Online]. Retrieved October 1, 2007 from www.csmonitor.com/soo6/0515/p13s01-stct.html

Gaudet, T. (2007). The power of laughter. *The Oprah Winfrey Show.*

Hanson, E. M. (1991). *Educational administration and organizational behavior.* Boston: Allyn & Bacon.

Hoy, W., & Miskel, C. (2001). *Educational administration: Theory, research, and practice* (6th ed.). Boston: McGraw-Hill.

Janis, I. L., & Mann, L. (1977). *Decision making: A psychological analysis of conflict, choice, and commitment.* New York: Free Press.

Lencioni, P. (2007). *Conquer team dysfunction.* Retrieved November 12, 2007, from http://www.tablegroup.com/pat/articles/article/?id=1

Novak, J. M. (2005). Invitational leadership. In B. Davies (Ed.) *The essentials of school leadership* (pp. 44-60). Thousand Oaks, CA: Sage.

Ohio State University Extension. (2000). *Building dynamic groups: Communication #4.* Retrieved October 1, 2007, from http://www.ag.ohio-state .edu/~bdg/pdf_docs/g/G04.pdf

Owen, J., & Ovando, M. (2000). *Superintendent's guide to creating community.* Lanham, MD: Scarecrow Press.

Patterson, J. L. (2007). Strengthening resilience in tough times. *NAESP Principal, 86*(5), 6-23.

Storey, V. (2001). Dean, judge, and bishop: Lessons from a conflict and implications for school leaders. *International Electronic Journal for Leadership in Learning, 5*(17). Retrieved August 1, 2004, from www.ucalgary.ca/~iejll/volume5/Storey.html

Thomas, K. (1976). Conflict and conflict management. In M. D. Dunnette (Ed.), *Handbook of industrial and organizational psychology* (pp. 889-936). Chicago: Rand McNally.

Thomas, K. (n.d.). *Managing conflict management a strategic advantage.* Retrieved January 17, 2008, from the Consulting Psychologist Press Web site: http://www.cpp.com/content/conflict_whitepaper.pdf

Notes

Notes